Author and Editor
Nick Pigott

Designer
Tim Pipes
Leanne Lawrence

Reprographics
Jonathan Schofield

Sub-Editor
Nigel Devereux

Group production editor
Tim Hartley

Production manager
Craig Lamb

Publisher
Dan Savage

Commercial director
Nigel Hole

Business development director
Terry Clark

Managing director
Brian Hill

Advertising
Carol Woods
cwoods@mortons.co.uk

Published by
Mortons Media Group Ltd, Media Centre,
Morton Way, Horncastle, Lincolnshire LN9 6JR
Tel: 01507 529529
All material copyright
Mortons Media Limited, 2012.
All rights reserved.

The Railway Magazine address: as above

Printed by:
William Gibbons & Son, Wolverhampton

ISBN 978-1-906167-82-0

The RAILWAY *Magazine*

A *Railway Magazine* Publication

MORTONS MEDIA GROUP LTD

Contents

Above: One of the most famous trains in British railway history was the 'Silver Jubilee', introduced in 1935 to mark the 25th anniversary of King George V. In 1977, British Rail took the happy decision to revive the title for Queen Elizabeth II's 25th anniversary and produced locomotive headboards bearing this ceremonial coat of arms

Facing page: The 'Big Four' companies made much use of art deco posters to promote their named expresses in the 1930s. This LMS artwork portrays the speed and glamour of 'The Coronation Scot'.

FRONT COVER: Clockwise from top left: The 'Golden Arrow' (with 35015 *Rotterdam Lloyd* at Sydenham Hill in April 1959); 'The Royal Scot' with 46223 *Princess Alice* at Glasgow Central in 1959; 'The Cheltenham Spa Express' (with 7035 *Ogmore Castle* at Purton in 1962); 'The Flying Scotsman' (with a 'Deltic' in 1964). R C RILEY, HUGH BALLANTYNE and COLOUR-RAIL.

Welcome to the glamorous world of

Named Expresses

FOR any enthusiast who fell in love with railways during the 1950s and early '60s, named expresses will almost certainly hold a fascination. Children's picture books in that era contained paintings and other colourful illustrations of famous trains such as 'The Royal Scot' and the 'Atlantic Coast Express' steaming through idyllic, sun-kissed countryside.

On some main lines, it was possible to witness a procession of headboards bearing names that hinted at romantic and glamorous far-off destinations, such as the 'Golden Arrow' and the 'Cornish Riviera'.

It was an exciting time to be a rail enthusiast and a rewarding time to be a passenger, for it was clear that the railways were going out of their way to add a touch of quality to an otherwise austere post-war scene.

This encyclopaedia is a fully revised, updated and enlarged version of a directory that appeared in *The Railway Magazine* as a four-part series over the winter of 2011/12 (issues 1,327, 1,329, 1,330 and 1,331). It contains numerous new photographs and several additional minor train names it was not possible to include in the previous series due to lack of space.

It is thus by far and away the most comprehensive directory of British titled trains ever published. The few books dedicated solely to the subject in the past have all featured only selections of trains, while other forms of media have compiled only lists, without descriptions.

This book contains no fewer than 360 seperate entries (well over 400 if the miscellaneous listings are included) and provides an invaluable record of Britain's railway heyday. It is also a celebration of the wonderful era when almost every major British city had its own prestige service to London. More often than not, the title of the train would reflect some aspect of that city's history or individuality (e.g. 'The Master Cutler' (Sheffield), 'The Mayflower' (Plymouth), 'The Robin Hood' (Nottingham), 'The Granite City' (Aberdeen) and 'The Mary Rose' (Portsmouth).

Then there were the Pullmans – opulent, prestigious, glamorous, luxurious. Until the early 1960s, these cars were privately owned and contained table lamps, curtains and polished veneer. They excited schoolboy spotters on the lineside and turned a train ride from a mere journey into an unforgettable experience.

The habit of referring to a train by a name dates

back to the 1840s with the 'Irish Mail' and the 'Flying Dutchman', but it wasn't until 1876 that the first officially-sanctioned train title appeared with the 'Granville Special Express'.

Even after that, it was to be several more decades before the idea of train-naming really took off in a big way in the 1920s.

The Railway Magazine has previous involvement in this subject, having helped the Great Western Railway name the 'Cornish Riviera Express' by way of an exclusive readers' competition in the Edwardian era, more than 100 years ago. It has also faithfully recorded the remarkable rise and fall of the train-naming phenomenon in Great Britain, there now being a mere handful of titles left in service.

Although carriage roofboards had been carried on some trains since the Victorian era, the physical attachment of a name to the front of a locomotive on a regular basis is not thought to have occured until a couple of years before the First World War when the North British Railway began attaching a headboard to

Picture on facing page: A remarkable collection of BR-style locomotive headboards on one of the walls of the National Railway Museum in York. Each colour represents a different Region of BR – red for the London Midland Region, dark blue for the Eastern and light blue for the Scottish. Missing from this particular display are brown Western Region and green Southern Region boards – the green of 'The Northern Irishman' being a one-off to reflect the national colour of the 'emerald isle' (although, surprisingly, 'The Emerald Isle Express' hasn't been so honoured!) Odd men out are 'The Condor' (a named freight train) and the charter train boards in the top two corners. Picture: CHRIS MILNER

the 'Fife Coast Express' and 'Lothian Coast Express'.

A few more trains began to be named (some only semi-officially), but the practice did not really begin to take off until the 1920s when the 'Flying Scotsman' – informally christened as far back as 1862 – was granted sanctioned status by the LNER by way of coach roofboards and a locomotive headboard.

The LNER, explaining that its decision was "partly to systemise unofficial references and partly to recognise and cultivate public interest", added 'The Aberdonian, the 'Night Scotsman' and the 'Scarborough Flyer' to its repertoire on January 1, 1927.

The LMS followed suit that summer and that started a welcome spate of train naming by all 'Big Four' companies… but it all came to a sudden halt in August/September 1939 with the outbreak of the Second World War. Only a tiny handful of trains retained their official identities during the conflict.

Although 1927 had seen more titles launched than any other year, the golden age was not the 1920s or '30s, but the British Railways era of the 1950s. In its first 12 years, BR doubled the number of named services by launching more than 40 new titles and relaunching many more. In so doing, it produced a new design of attractive curved-edged headboards and the regular use of such embellishments on all six BR Regions provided the nation's crack expresses with a much higher public profile.

The headboards that identified those trains have come to mean a lot to the generation of enthusiasts who grew up with them and such embellishments now change hands for substantial sums at railwayana auctions. One of the finest displays of plates can be seen covering an entire wall at the National Railway Museum (see picture above).

Although a nationalised industry, BR didn't enforce rigid standardisation on this aspect of its business and allowed the Southern Region (and to a lesser extent the London Midland) to have rectangular and circular headboards too.

Today, most of that colourful character has been

Above: An idyllic late-1950s scene in south Devon as 47XX 2-8-0 No. 4704 skirts the coast with 'The Royal Duchy'. Of such images are memories made. Painting by MALCOLM ROOT

lost from the railways, largely because of the intensive use of fixed formation rolling stock. No longer is it possible to keep an expensive set of coaches aside for just one or two journeys a day; trains are more standardised and must be able to deputise for a classmates at short notice. They're also often uniformly timed these days, so have no claim to a distinctive name that would set them apart from their slower brethren.

It's certainly an increasingly anonymous railway now, yet not all train operating companies have

forgotten how it used to be and several, notably First Great Western, have retained some of the historic names – although today, of course, there are no headboards and the only way of telling a named train from any other is via small adhesive window labels or tiny timetable footnotes.

A modern equivalent of the titled train is the 'branded service', of which 'Stansted Express' and 'Gatwick Express' are examples.

This 'bookazine' includes all types of name (pointing out which are which), thereby listing virtually

A NEW INTERCITY EXPRESS

The Royal Duchy

Fridays only from 15 May 1987

THE FASTEST EVER TRAIN FROM LONDON TO PENZANCE
4hrs:46min

≥ InterCity *21*

In the late 1980s, 'The Royal Duchy' was relaunched as an HST diesel service, but the image was of a much brasher nature than that of 30 years earlier.

every title seen on the main lines of Britain from the 1840s to the present day.

The temptation to take the easy option and exclude all unofficial, generic and brand titles has been resisted because the book is intended to answer the initial queries of anyone wishing to make a general inquiry into the subject and it's therefore as important to state what was *not* an official titled train as to say what was.

However, the subject generally is a minefield of complexity and it is beyond the remit of this publication to go into the full timetabling history of each train (such

a book – even if possible to compile – would take years and years of frustrating research and probably result in an extremely dry and boring read!)

It must be borne in mind that national all-line timetables didn't always mention every train name and that several were printed only in local booklets or publicity material. As the latter have not survived in such great numbers as the national timetables, it is almost impossible after all these years to pin down exact dates (especially finishing dates, as launches were often accompanied by a formal announcement or ceremony, whereas cessation of usage often simply petered out).

Neither did timetable entries always correspond, date-wise, with the use of headboards or carriage window labels, so although great care has been taken to ensure that discrepancies are kept to a minimum, some dates are unavoidably approximate.

There is, however, the question of what exactly was a titled train? In the post-war steam and early diesel era, it is pretty clear-cut and even in the 1920s and 30s some order was emerging from the timetables – but in the modern era, the use of brand names has muddied the waters, while in the pre-Grouping era, the

Although the majority of photographs in this publication unavoidably feature steam age scenes, diesel and electric traction is very much part of the titled train story and there are numerous illustrations depicting such motive power. This is 'Deltic' No. D9013 *The Black Watch* at King's Cross with 'The Flying Scotsman' in May 1963. COLOUR-RAIL

subject is riddled with even more confusion.

There were, for example, many discrepancies between Bradshaw's timetables and the railway companies' own literature and timetables.

It is also a moot point as to how the Victorians and Edwardians differentiated between a train title and what was merely a train description.

Into the latter category could be placed such phrases as 'Limited Mail' and 'Scotch Express', but for the purposes of this encyclopaedia, it has been decided to include as much nomenclature as possible whilst making it clear whether it was likely to have been a description or a brand name.

Although it makes for a fascinating perusal, it is not necessary to read this book from cover to cover as it's intended primarily for use as a reference source – hopefully to be kept as an at-a-glance guide for many years to come.

NOTES ON THE USE OF THIS BOOK:
First of all, it is necessary to point out that the history of titled trains is a jungle of confusion and contradictory evidence. Even headboards, roofboards, timetables and publicity material frequently disagreed with each other (often within the same railway company even), as did the work of respected authors and researchers - most of whom have concentrated on a particular timeframe or specific technical or geographic aspect of the subject. Departure times and calling points have changed so much over the years that we would be on a hiding-to-nothing to try including them all, so only those that remained reasonably consistent have been left in.

It has been necessary to use a number of explanatory devices in the main directory:
- Brackets around the word 'The' in some train titles indicate that official use of the definite article varied during the train's existence and that both versions were used.
- Brackets around the whole title mean that the service was not an individual named train in the normally-accepted sense but a brand name or generic fleet description.
- The use of single inverted commas around a heading only (i.e. not in general text) refers to an unofficial title. This, however does not apply to train titles in the Victorian era or the first couple of decades of the 20th century, as formal sanctioning of titles by railway companies did not become commonplace until the 1920s.
- Double inverted commas indicates a nickname.
- An asterisk after a name indicates that the title is in use in 2012.

As a general rule, times of steam age services are in a.m. and p.m., while those of the more modern era are in

Below: A Class 09 shunter is not a type of loco one would expect to find in a book on titled trains, but this rare photo shows one engaged in the process of shunting the stock of the 'Night Ferry' into the ship's hold at Dover. The 'Night Ferry' was the only train whose coaches ran on both sides of the English Channel.

Two of the most glamorous titles side-by-side on the smokebox doors of 'Merchant Navy' Pacifics at south London's Stewarts Lane depot in the 1950s. The 'Golden Arrow' and the 'Night Ferry' were unusual in retaining large circular headboards for most of the BR steam era. R C RILEY

24-hour clock style. (The actual adoption of the latter on BR was June 1965 but a little flexibility either way has been allowed).

'Limited' in the context of a train title indicates that seating was limited and that advance booking was therefore necessary.

The following types of trains are not included in the main directory, but are listed in self-contained text panels:

Ocean liner boat trains from London Waterloo to Southampton; North-West club trains, holiday trains; land cruises; named freight trains… plus a selection of foreign named expresses.

Most preservation era titles (railtours, charters and main line specials such as the 'Cumbrian Mountain Express') have also been excluded from the main directory, which concentrates primarily on timetabled pubic services.

Also excluded are out-and-out nicknames such as "Lancing Belle", "Beeswing" and "Annesley Dido" as the list would be frankly endless – although it has been decided to include a few unofficial and colloquial titles (which may or may not have been construed as nicknames by some people over the years).

So entangled and entwined is the jungle that it's no surprise that so few attempts have been made to tame it. We feel that this bookazine, whilst not perfect, is the nearest anyone has come to doing so.

For help in trying to bring order to the confusion, I would particularly like to thank the following: Charles Long (for valuable advice on Pullman services), David Hull (for information on services in the post-headboard era and, in particular, for providing many of the window labels that help illustrate the text); G J Child, Malcolm Whitby, David Percival, Keith Farr,

Alex Owen, Chris Milner, Doug Beecher and Michael Donovan.

Last but not least, our thanks to *The Railway Magazine* readers who kindly submitted observations and updates on the original four-part survey. Readers wishing to delve further into specific trains are recommended to Cecil J Allen's 'Titled Trains of Great Britain' (Ian Allan) and Dave Peel's 'Locomotive Headboards (Sutton Publishing).

If despite all of the foregoing, readers feel they need to point out any discrepancies, they are invited to write to or email me at *The Railway Magazine*, whose address appears on page 3.

Many thanks
NICK PIGOTT

Below: The pre-preservation equivalent of the photo on pages 4 and 5: Depots at which express engines were frequently changed often possessed headboard repositories, such as this one at Grantham on the Eastern Region.
GAVIN MORRISON

THE ABERDONIAN

ABERDEEN

via
Darlington   Stonehaven
Newcastle   Edinburgh
Kirkcaldy   Dundee
Arbroath   Montrose

Above: The very first entry in the A to Z of titled trains is the 'Aberdonian', seen waiting to depart from its home city on August 6, 1935. The loco is P2 class 2-8-2 No. 2002 Earl Marischal, one of a class of powerful engines built the previous year to eliminate the uneconomical practice of double-heading on the taxing Aberdeen-Edinburgh route.
W YEADON COLLECTION

(THE) ABERDONIAN

THE origins of 'The Aberdonian' lay in the unofficial 'race to Aberdeen', which was contested by the East and West Coast companies in 1895 in a bid to achieve the fastest time between London and the 'Granite City'. The contest was won by the West Coast with an astonishing time of 512 minutes for 540 miles, including three stops, but it was as an East Coast express that 'The Aberdonian' was to make its name.

Its operation in the early days was shared between the Great Northern, North Eastern and North British railways, but it wasn't until the London & North Eastern Railway (LNER) had taken over those three companies in the 1923 Grouping that the train was afforded an official name.

The first titled run of this prestigious sleeping car service took place on July 11, 1927, and it contained dining car facilities and through portions for places such as Inverness and Fort William. By the 1930s, it had grown to become an extremely heavy train, so much so that a 7.25pm summers-only relief service had to be laid on (confusingly with a completely different name – see 'The Highlandman'). It was in that section that the Inverness, Fort William and Nairn sleeping car portions were contained, the latter detached at Aviemore. That train was followed out of King's Cross at 7.40pm by 'The Aberdonian' itself, which contained through sections for Elgin and Lossiemouth.

Right: In BR days, 'The Aberdonian' (now with the addition of the definite article) leaves Aberdeen in the charge of A2 No 60532 Blue Peter on June 25, 1957. BRIAN MORRISON

The train was almost always hauled by Pacifics between London and Edinburgh but, on the twisting Aberdeen road in the 1930s, would normally be handled by Gresley P2 2-8-2 locomotives specially designed for such duties.

'The Aberdonian' was one of only four British trains to retain its title throughout the Second World War, although for security reasons the headboards and carriage boards were not actually carried during the hostilities. In the early

1960s, by which time it had grown to more than 500 tons and been switched to diesel traction, the departure time of its up working was altered to 8.30pm and, from 1971 to 1982, a 10.15pm service from King's Cross carried the title 'The Night Aberdonian'.

In 1971, 'The Aberdonian' proper ceased to be an overnight sleeping car train when its title was transferred again, this time to a 12noon down departure and a 10.30am from the 'Granite City'.

This daylight 'Aberdonian' became an HST working in the summer of 1979, although the lack of a headboard on the new form of traction took much of the glamour away and to all intents and purposes, rendered it an ordinary train identifiable only by paper window stickers.

Probably the most surprising alteration took place with the 1982 summer timetable change, when the time-honoured 10am departure from King's Cross – which had for more than 100 years been the time slot of 'The Flying Scotsman' – was handed by BR to 'The Aberdonian', thus ending more than a century of history. The southbound 'Aberdonian' also began its journey at 10am, but not for long, for in October of that year, it was all-change again as the departure time of the up service was altered to 8.40am. The name continued to be used, off and on, until summer 1994, when the train was replaced by the 'Northern Lights'.

■ For details of the 'Aberdeen-Penzance' service, see 'The Cornishman'.

THE ADMIRAL DE RUYTER

INTRODUCED by British Rail in May 1987, this was the 09.40 Liverpool Street to Harwich Parkeston Quay boat train and 19.40 return. Because the ferries it connected with sailed for Amsterdam, the service was named after a Dutch naval commander who led a raid on the Medway ports in June 1667 during the Second Anglo-Dutch War.

It is interesting to note that two versions of the title existed, one in English and one in Dutch (the latter the same except for the spelling of the first word – Admiraal).

Until May 1987, the service had been called 'The Day Continental'. By 1989, the title had been dropped, although the service – one of only two BR trains to gain Euro-City Express status – continued to run.

'THE AFGHAN'

A NAME coined in 1879 to describe the Great Western Railway's 4.45pm Paddington-Wolverhampton service between London and Didcot. The appellation was necessary to differentiate it from another GWR train, 'The Zulu', which was launched the same day in June of that year. After leaving Didcot, the Wolverhampton train became known as 'The Northern Zulu'.

Although both names were unofficial, this is believed to be the only case of a train changing names in mid-journey. Both titles commemorated wars being waged at the time of their namings – 'The Afghan' referring to the Second Anglo-Afghan War, which lasted from 1878 to 1880. (The Anglo-Zulu War was fought in 1879).

THE AFTERNOON CALEDONIAN

IN 1958, the frequency of the West Coast express 'The Caledonian' was doubled and between June 9 and September 12 that year, 'The Morning Caledonian' and 'The Afternoon Caledonian' were in operation, although the wording on the locomotive headboards remained unchanged. 'The Afternoon Caledonian' left Glasgow at 4pm.

THE AFTERNOON TALISMAN

BR doubled the frequency of 'The Talisman' East Coast express in 1957 and, for that summer and the duration of the September 1958 to June 1959 timetable, the services were referred to in timetables as 'The Morning Talisman' and 'The Afternoon Talisman', although the original loco headboards continued to be used. Departure time from both King's Cross and Edinburgh for 'The Afternoon Talismans' was 4pm. The reason for the gap in the dates was that from September 1957 to September 1958, the 'Morning Talisman' ran as 'The Fair Maid'.

(AIRDRIE EXPRESS)

(*Brand name*): An electric multiple unit service in operation between Glasgow Queen Street and Airdrie, mid-1980s.

'THE ALTCAR BOB'

THIS strange epithet, possibly a nickname, was used to describe a Railmotor service run by the Lancashire & Yorkshire Railway (and later the LMS) from Southport to Altcar & Hillhouse between 1906 and 1938.

'AMERICAN CAR TRAIN'

(*Descriptive term*). See ' Folkestone Vestibule Limited'.

ANTWERP CONTINENTAL

THIS was one of several 'Continental' boat trains run from

ANGLO-SCOTTISH CAR CARRIER

Motor cars by rail: A4 No. 60032 *Gannet* with headboard at Newcastle in May 1960. COLOUR-RAIL

Letting the train take the strain

ALTHOUGH its name might suggest that it was a freight train, this was an express passenger service, often hauled by an A4 Pacific. It was inaugurated as a named train on May 30, 1960, and ran as a day-time seated accommodation version of the 'Car Sleeper Limited', containing passenger coaches plus car-carrying wagons.

Because the cars couldn't be loaded at King's Cross passenger station, the operation was carried out at Holloway, a mile north of the terminus.

In 1962, the train gained purpose-built double-decker car-carrying vehicles. Departure was 7.55am on weekdays and it arrived in Edinburgh Waverley at 3.18pm with the return leaving the latter at 12.55 for an 8.30 arrival in Holloway.

Thought to be the only such train to regularly carry a headboard, it was 'Deltic'-hauled on occasions and made its last run on September 24, 1966.

London by the LNER to connect with ships at Harwich Parkeston Quay. The others were the 'Day Continental', the 'Flushing Continental' and the 'Hook Continental'.

In LNER days, the train grew in popularity and on some days could gross more than 400 tons… a tough challenge for B12 and B17 4-6-0s and their crews.

The origins of the services date back to the Great Eastern Railway, which had been running boat trains since the end of the 19th century and which, from February 1921, began to attach a Pullman car to the 'Antwerp Continental', which left London at 8.40pm in order to connect with the ferry's night sailing. The up train left Parkeston Quay at 6.32am. In that first year, the train was known as the 'Antwerp Express' in the down direction and the 'Continental Express' when running to London.

(For the purposes of this encyclopaedia, we have placed into a different section [p27] the boat trains run to Southampton and other large ports in connection with the sailings of ocean-going liners because those ran only on certain days 'as required', whereas the Harwich ferry-boat trains were regular timetabled services.)

Unlike the 'Hook Continental', the morning down 'Antwerp Continental' used to continue to Dovercourt Bay and Harwich Town and therefore wasn't purely a boat train, but it did for a while convey non-supplementary fare Pullman cars. During the period of the 'Great Depression' in Britain, the two services were merged and ran as the 'Hook & Antwerp Continental' between July 1932 and July 1937. The 'Antwerp Continental' reappeared in July 1946 but had ceased altogether by 1954.

(THE) ATLANTIC COAST EXPRESS *

THE Atlantic Coast Express, or 'ACE' as it was often referred to, was one of the most complicated services in terms of portions and route permutations. Woe betide any passenger who inadvertently sat in the wrong part of this train!

At its peak, it included no fewer than nine sections in its formation and has been described by the eminent railway author Cecil J Allen as "the most multi-portioned train in the country".

Anyone visiting Waterloo for its mid-morning departure in the 1930s would find nearest the locomotive the Ilfracombe section, usually consisting of three coaches, followed by portions for Torrington, Padstow, Bude and Plymouth, then a two-coach restaurant car section (to be detached at Exeter) and behind that portions for Exmouth, Sidmouth and Seaton.

The Seaton portion would be the first to be detached, at Salisbury, going forward behind a stopping train that followed the main express. At Sidmouth Junction, the Sidmouth and Exmouth sections were taken off and worked to their respective destinations by tank engines.

Next stop for the main train was Exeter Central, where the restaurant cars (which by that time had become the rear vehicles), were shunted off and the remaining carriages were divided into two trains and given a fresh engine each. One would run to Barnstaple Junction, where it would drop off the Torrington section and pick up the Ilfracombe-bound through coach of the Great Western Railway's 'Cornish Riviera', which had been dropped off at Taunton and worked forward from there.

The joint SR-GWR train would then continue to the north Devon resort of Ilfracombe, while the Torrington section departed along the short section to that town.

Meanwhile, back in Exeter, the remaining sections set off for Okehampton, where the Padstow and Bude coaches were shunted off. They were then worked forward to Halwill Junction, where they were divided yet again for their respective north Cornish resorts, while the Plymouth section went forward from Okehampton. By the time the Padstow portion arrived at its destination, passengers had been travelling for more than 6½ hours and had covered some 260 miles since leaving London – the longest through journey on Southern metals.

So popular was the 'ACE' in the summer holiday seasons that it sometimes had to be despatched from Waterloo in as many as five separate trains, four of them being relief trains run in advance of the main departure.

The 'ACE' made its maiden journey as a named train on July 19, 1926,

its title having been chosen in a competition open to Southern Railway staff to find a name for the 11am departure from Waterloo. It was usually powered by SR 4-6-0s of the 'Lord Nelson' and 'King Arthur' classes but, from the 1940s onwards, Bulleid Pacifics took over the fast Waterloo-Exeter section, with Moguls or Light Pacifics having charge west of Exeter.

The train was suspended during the Second World War but enjoyed a post-war revival under BR in the 1950s and, at least between London and Exeter, became one of the nation's crack expresses.

But it was to prove an Indian summer, for several of the branch lines on which its portions ran were gradually closed and the whole of the Southern's lines west of Exeter were then transferred to 'the old enemy', the Western, and thereafter the writing was on the wall. Portions were gradually withdrawn and the 'ACE' itself was killed off as a named train on September 5, 1964.

The title was briefly revived by British Rail InterCity in 1988 for a London-Newquay summer service (ironically departing from Paddington)... and there is still a train of the same name on the Newquay line today, operated by First Great Western. It was resurrected in the early years of Privatisation by FGW's predecessor and, since 2008, has been running as a short-dated weekday summer service (early July to early September), aimed primarily at the holiday market. It operates on summer weekdays as the 09.06 Paddington-Newquay HST, returning from the Cornish resort at 15.00. (Saturday times are 11.35 and 11.22 respectively)

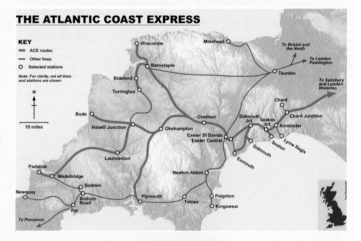

THE ATLANTIC COAST EXPRESS

KEY
- ACE routes
- Other lines
- ○ Selected stations

Note: For clarity, not all lines and stations are shown

Above: A map showing the numerous destinations of the 'Atlantic Coast Express'.

Left: Although the portions for Seaton, Sidmouth and Exmouth were detached in advance, Exeter was the main dividing junction for the 'ACE'. 'Merchant Navy' No. 35025 *Brocklebank Line* leaves Exeter Central with the up train circa 1952.
RAIL PHOTOPRINTS

ANTWERP EXPRESS
See entry on page 11.

THE ARMADA *
RECALLING the Spanish armada defeated off the coast of Plymouth in 1588, this title was coined by British Rail's Cross-Country sector in May 1988 to identify the 06.09 Leeds-Plymouth and 06.30 Plymouth-York HST diagram.

By 1997/98, the itinerary had changed to 06.05 York-Plymouth and 06.20 Plymouth-Newcastle, but the name sank from the national timetable in 2002 before being salvaged by First Great Western in December 2011 for the 05.53 Plymouth-Paddington and 19.03 return, extended to Penzance on Fridays.

ATLANTIC HERITAGE
A NAME given by BR ScotRail in 1991 to the 12.27 Inverness-Kyle of Lochalsh service and 17.00 return. The title was dropped in September 1992.

AYRSHIRE TRADER
THIS train was unusual in bearing different titles for its out and back services.

Introduced by BR's ScotRail sector in winter 1989/90, the 'Ayrshire Trader' was the 17.00 Newcastle-Girvan service, whereas the return 06.45 Girvan-Newcastle was known as the 'Tyne Trader'.

Both services were operated by Class 156 'Super Sprinters' and the titles were dropped in winter 1997/98.

BALLATER EXPRESS
ONE of a handful of named trains run by the Great North of Scotland Railway, this one linked Ballater with Aberdeen and ran during the first two decades of the 20th century.

BELFAST BOAT EXPRESS
TRAINS of this name ran on three different routes:
1) between London Paddington and Birkenhead in GWR days to connect with Liverpool-Belfast night sailings,
2) between London Euston and Fleetwood Harbour via the West Coast Main Line, and 3) from Manchester Victoria to Heysham Harbour, also connecting with Belfast steamers.

In the late 1960s, the latter became the last steam-hauled named train on British Rail. The service continued into the diesel era but ceased running on the day the Heysham ferry was withdrawn, April 6, 1975.

THE BENJAMIN BRITTEN
A SHORT-LIVED name introduced by British Rail in 1987 to describe the 07.45 Harwich Parkeston Quay to London Liverpool Street 'Euro-City Express' service and 19.50 return. The train, named after the famous British composer, also appeared in the 1988 timetable with slightly amended times, but had been dropped by October 1989.

BLACKPOOL & FYLDE COAST EXPRESS
THIS was a short-lived title for a service put on by the London Midland & Scottish Railway in 1934 to provide the popular resort of Blackpool with a daily link to London.

Leaving the Lancashire resort at around 8.25am, it

Above: British Railways' very last steam-hauled titled train was the 'Belfast Boat Express'. This May 1968 picture shows the final working being greeted by the sun as it arrives in Manchester Victoria behind a suitably-cleaned 'Black Five', No. 45025. Work-stained classmate No. 45255 pays its last respects.
COLOUR-RAIL

(THE) BIRMINGHAM PULLMAN

One of the Metro-Cammell eight-car units stands at Birmingham Snow Hill station. Note the Pullman coat of arms on the front. This was a specially elongated re-working of the one on the back cover of this publication.

Pullman DMUs – a new look for an old favourite

THIS was one of British Railways' famous 'Blue Pullman' diesel trains (see also 'Bristol Pullman', 'Midland Pullman', 'Oxford Pullman' and 'South Wales Pullman').

They were the first and only diesel multiple unit Pullmans in the country and also featured a striking blue & white livery instead of the time-honoured umber & cream.

Unlike locomotive-hauled Pullman cars, these self-propelled traction units were not exclusively owned by the Pullman Car Co, but jointly owned with British Railways from their introduction in 1960 until completion of the purchase of the Pullman Car Company by the British Transport Commission in 1962.

Metropolitan-Cammell built three eight-car sets for the Western Region and each was powered by North British/MAN 1,000hp diesel-electric power cars.

Unlike their Midland Region sisters (two six-car sets), the WR examples never carried their full service names on the bodysides, although their titles were publicised on bodyside roller-blinds and in publicity literature. They also carried first and second-class passengers, whereas the six-car sets were first-class only.

The 'Birmingham Pullman' was introduced on the same day as the 'Bristol Pullman' and ran a daily return journey from Wolverhampton Low Level, calling at Birmingham Snow Hill, Solihull and Leamington. Instead of lying over in London, it made an additional return trip to Birmingham in the middle of the day.

By March 1967, electrification of the West Coast Main Line had brought about such an improvement in London Euston to Birmingham New Street timings that the Western Region route from Paddington to Snow Hill was reduced in status, with the result that the two diesel units were transferred to other WR routes.

The last 'Blue Pullman' services were discontinued in 1973 with the Western Region's decision to condemn the entire fleet of trains. None of the units survive – but, following the general relaunch of the Pullman name by BR as an upmarket brand in 1985, the 'Birmingham Pullman' title was reinstated in 1987/8 for a loco-hauled Euston-Birmingham New Street-Wolverhampton 'InterCity Shuttle' service, which was perpetuated by Virgin Trains until 1998.

would arrive in the capital at lunchtime, with the down train setting off at around 5pm to ensure Fylde coast residents reached home some five hours later.

The train was a mini version of the Southern's 'Atlantic Coast Express', containing a restaurant service and making stops at Wigan and Preston for through coaches to and from Blackburn, Burnley, Colne and Barrow.

It lost its title upon the outbreak of war in 1939 and never regained it.

(BLUE PULLMAN)

(*Brand name*): A generic term for a fleet of Pullman DMUs. See under separate entries – 'Birmingham Pullman', 'Bristol Pullman', 'Midland Pullman', 'Oxford Pullman', 'South Wales Pullman'.

THE BON ACCORD

THIS was one of two expresses introduced by the LMS on July 5, 1937, to cover the 153-mile Glasgow-Aberdeen run in just three hours (the other was 'The Saint Mungo').

Departing Glasgow Buchanan Street at 10.05 and usually hauled by one of the then new 'Jubilee' 4-6-0s, it was limited to eight coaches (including a restaurant car) in order to maintain the demanding schedule over difficult terrain.

The train's name – which is the motto of the city of Aberdeen – was discontinued a week after the outbreak of war, on September 8, 1939, but resurrected by BR 10 years later, on May 23, 1949 – albeit for a different service, the 6.25am from Aberdeen and 1.35pm ex-Buchanan Street.

From June 1962, it was used to describe the 7.10am Aberdeen-Glasgow and 2.05pm return (12.05pm on Saturdays). Upon closure of Buchanan Street on November 7, 1966, the train used Glasgow Queen Street.

The last run as a titled train took place on May 4, 1968, eight months to the day after closure to passengers of the ex-Caledonian main line between Stanley Jct and Kinnaber Jct, although by then, the headboards had long ceased to be carried by the locos.

THE BORDERER

THIS name appeared for the first time in the BR timetable of winter 1989/90 and was applied to the 15.54 Glasgow Central-Newcastle service that ran to Carlisle via the ex-Glasgow & South Western route through Kilmarnock and Dumfries. Operated by ScotRail Class 156 'Super Sprinter', it ceased as a titled train at the end of the summer 1996 timetable.

(THE) BOURNEMOUTH BELLE

PERHAPS by virtue of their attractive feminine suffixes, the 'Belles' of the Southern were among the most-loved of all Britain's named trains.

One of the best-known was the 'Bournemouth Belle', born on July 5, 1931.

At first it ran as a seven-days-week operation only in summer, leaving London Waterloo at 10am and running non-stop to Southampton West and Bournemouth Central, where a five-car portion was detached for Weymouth. During the winter, the train ran on Sundays only, but, in January 1936, it began to operate on an all-year-round daily basis with a halt at Southampton Central (which had been renamed from Southampton West the previous year). The Weymouth portion had

been discontinued after the first season.

The train was all-Pullman from the start and consisted of between seven and 10 first and third class cars, some of which were 12-wheelers. Haulage was usually entrusted to a 'Lord Nelson' or 'King Arthur' class 4-6-0.

As with many luxury trains, it was withdrawn at the outbreak of war but reinstated on October 7, 1946, by which time 'Merchant Navy' Pacifics were available for motive power. This enabled the formation to be increased to 10 or even 12 vehicles.

In 1965, Bournemouth West station was closed and the train terminated at the town's Central station for the final months of its existence, which came to an end in July 1967, there being no electric Pullman units available for the South-Western division of the SR.

BOURNEMOUTH LIMITED

A WATERLOO-Bournemouth express that wasn't formally named until July 1929 but had its roots in a non-stop service operated between those two locations by the London & South Western Railway from 1899.

The departure times of the named train were 7.42am from Bournemouth and 4.30pm from Waterloo. It contained restaurant facilities and through coaches for Weymouth and Swanage, which were detached at Bournemouth.

'The Limited' was withdrawn at the onset of the Second World War and, unlike the 'Bournemouth Belle', was never reinstated, although an all-new express was introduced along the same route in 1945 and later became 'The Royal Wessex'.

BRADFORD EXECUTIVE

IN the years preceding the squadron introduction of HSTs in the late-1970s, the Eastern Region of BR marketed a service by the name of 'High Speed' on the East Coast Main Line using 'Deltic' Type 5s and Brush Type 4s coupled to short

(eight-vehicle) rakes of Mk 2 coaches.

Although limited to 100mph, such dining car-equipped trains could maintain high speeds for longer, especially if run non-stop, and were thus ideal for business executives and other long-distance commuters.

In 1971, air-conditioned updated versions of Mk 2s were introduced and, two years later, the trains began to receive official names.

The 'Bradford Executive' was one of the first three (the others being the 'Leeds Executive' and the 'Newcastle Executive') and by 1978 it was completing the journey between London and the West Riding in less than 2½ hours, but those times were eclipsed when the 125mph 'High-Speed Trains' began to arrive on the ECML from 1978, slashing almost 20 minutes off some of the schedules.

At various times of its existence, the service has been formed of loco-hauled stock (both diesel and electric) and HST and has used both Bradford stations, Forster Square and Exchange/Interchange.

The train had disappeared from the timetable by May 1990.

THE BRADFORD PULLMAN

CONTRARY to popular opinion, Britain's first Pullman service – run by the Midland Railway from London to Bradford in June 1874 – was never named. However, the title is included in this encyclopaedia by virtue of the fact that British Rail InterCity used it in July 1991 to describe the 06.46 Bradford Forster Square-King's Cross service and 15.50 return. It ran for only a year (although the 'Yorkshire Pullman' also used Forster Square at times over the following decade).

(BRIGHTON EXPRESS)

(*Brand name*): A Class 319 electric multiple unit service ran on the Brighton line under this name in the 1980s/90s.

Top of page: With a long rake of umber & cream Pullmans in tow, rebuilt 'Merchant Navy' No. 35016 *Elders Fyffes* eases past the back yards south of Clapham Junction with the 'Bournemouth Belle' on September 10, 1961.
R C RILEY

Above: How the Southern Railway advertised the 'Bournemouth Belle' in the art deco style of the 1930s. The service ran on Sundays-only until the end of 1935.

BRIGHTON BELLE

Beautiful belles

ON the last day of 1932, the Southern Railway withdrew the steam-hauled Pullman rolling stock of the 'Southern Belle' and replaced it the following day with a brand new electric multiple unit train.

The first motor-driven Pullman cars in the world, the new five-car units – usually coupled together to form ten-coach sets – began operating three return journeys every weekday from London Victoria to Brighton, departing the capital at 11am, 3pm and 7pm.

After a year and a half, the SR decided to change the name of the train from 'Southern Belle' to 'Brighton Belle' to bring it into line with the 'Bournemouth Belle', which had been introduced in 1931 (and was just as much a 'Southern' belle in its own right). This name change took effect on June 29, 1934.

The outbreak of the Second World War in 1939 saw the EMUs withdrawn but they were subsequently reinstated until May 1942 when they were suspended "for the duration". They reappeared after October 7, 1946.

For most of its life, the 'BB' had been a London-based operation, but in 1963 it was switched to Brighton and given an additional up morning working, making four return trips a day. In 1967, the journey time was reduced to 55 minutes.

The British Transport Commission's acquisition of the Pullman Car Company in 1962, followed by BR's obsession with corporate identity during the 'blue era' that started in the mid-'60s, saw the attractive umber & cream Pullman livery replaced by grey & blue towards the end of that decade and the opportunity was taken to refurbish the carriages' tired interiors. But the makeover did little to boost the train's popularity and its dedicated rolling stock made it more and more of an anachronism on an increasingly-standardised rail system.

Life-expired, the units were put out of their misery on April 30, 1972.

More than a quarter of a century later, in May 1998, the famous name made a surprise reappearance in the BR timetable when it was adopted for the 16.52 Sundays-only service from Brighton to Victoria and 18.02 return. It was in use in 1998 and 1999 but although the service continued, the title had been dropped by summer 2000.

By the early 1970s, the traditional umber & cream Pullman company livery had been replaced on the units by British Rail's corporate blue & grey. Set No. 3052 is seen at Clapham Junction in 1969. Note that the coat of arms has been replaced by the train's name. CHRIS MILNER COLLECTION

Top of page: 'Brighton Belle' set No. 3051 makes its stately way between Victoria and the South Coast in earlier BR days.

'BRIGHTON LIMITED'

See 'Pullman Limited Express'.

BRIGHTON PULLMAN LIMITED

VARIOUSLY known also as the 'Brighton Limited' or the 'Pullman Limited' and with a full title of 'The Brighton Sunday Pullman Limited', this train was one of the first in the south of England to carry a name and came into existence on October 2, 1898 (the year before the 'Granville Express' stopped running).

The train could trace its origins back to the 'Pullman Limited Express' of 1881 and was specifically geared to the winter 'Brighton season', so did

not run in July, August or September.

First class only, it left London Victoria at 11am and was on the south coast an hour later – a time that was to be slashed dramatically to just 48 minutes in a test run on July 26, 1903, hauled by a Billinton 4-4-0.

Despite the potential shown by that outstanding performance, no general speed-up of the service was made, but the overall success of the 'Brighton Limited' proved to the railway's managers that there was scope for a daily service and a special train of seven 12-wheel coaches was ordered. Thus was born 'The Southern Belle', introduced in November 1908, from which date the Sundays-only train ceased to operate.

THE BRISTOLIAN *

THE centenary of the Great Western Railway in 1935 saw the company introduce a high-speed non-stop express on the London-Bristol main line.

The GWR already had titled trains, notably the 'Cornish Riviera' and 'Cheltenham Spa' expresses, but 'The Bristolian' was limited to seven purpose-built coaches and with a 'Castle' or 'King' at the head could be whisked to Bristol Temple Meads at an average speed approaching 70mph. It began on September 9, 1935, leaving Paddington at 10am and setting off from Bristol at 4.30, but, in common with many glamorous non-stop trains, was withdrawn just four years later for the duration of the war, not being reinstated as a named train until summer 1951.

One of the reasons for delaying the revival was that the timings had been slowed considerably by the hostilities and the Western Region did not feel it right to restore the name until the schedule was worthy, but the timings were gradually accelerated and by June 1954 were back to pre-war levels.

By the end of that decade, the first diesel-hydraulics had entered traffic and 100-minute schedules at an average speed of 80mph became possible, but instead of taking advantage of that, BR decided in 1961 to increase the loading of 'The Bristolian' to 10 or 11 coaches and add a stop at Bath Spa, thus ending the train's famous non-stop reputation.

The 'Warship' diesels perpetuated the classic nature of the named trains by carrying headboards in those early days of modernisation, but the writing was on the wall for titled trains generally and 'The Bristolian' lost its name in everything but timetable references on June 12, 1965. It was restored in 1971 but dropped again two years later.

In 1998, the name was revived and is today used on the 06.49 Weston-super-Mare to Paddington and the

THE BRISTOLIAN
London Paddington – Bristol Temple Meads
Bristol Temple Meads – London Paddington
Celebrating 175 Years of the Great Western Railway
www.vintagetrains.co.uk

18.00 Paddington-Bristol Temple Meads, both First Great Western HST workings.

(THE) BRITANNIA

FROM summer 1989, this was the name applied to the 18.35 Harwich Parkeston Quay to Manchester Piccadilly and the 07.05 Derby to Harwich services, the Derby start probably being to avoid empty stock moves.

The service was operated by British Rail's Provincial sector under its 'Express' branding, but the title was dropped at the start of the 1991 summer timetable.

**Above: In full cry...
'The Bristolian' heads westbound at Thingley Junction, near Chippenham, in the charge of a 'King' class 4-6-0 No. 6006 *King George I* in 1954. COLOUR-RAIL**

In their later years, the 'Blue Pullmans' ceased to be all-blue, exchanging their liveries for a predominantly grey colour scheme with full yellow ends, as seen on this 'Bristol Pullman' set near Keynsham in March 1973. RAIL PHOTOPRINTS

The earlier blue & white livery featuring the Pullman emblem. Note the driver's special white cap. COLOUR-RAIL

BRISTOL PULLMAN

THIS was one of the first two 'Blue Pullman' diesel trains to be launched on the Western Region (see 'Birmingham Pullman' for general background) and was inaugurated on September 12, 1960.

Like its sister Pullman trains, it shared a small fleet of three 8-car diesel multiple units, which operated on the WR for more than a decade.

In the years leading up to the launch of the 'Blue Pullmans', many prestigious services left London in the morning and returned in

the evening, but by 1960, the railway authorities had realised that increasing numbers of businessmen wanted to travel to London in the morning and vice versa, so the timings were arranged to enable the new trains to start to fill that need.

The 'Bristol Pullman' was intensively deployed, making two return journeys a day over the 118-mile route to Paddington via Bath (via Badminton until October 14, 1960), and it ceased to exist in 1973 when the fleet of special DMUs was condemned

'Britannia' No. 70009 *Alfred the Great* storms along the electrified section of the Great Eastern Main Line with 'The Broadsman' in the late-1950s.
Painting by MALCOLM ROOT

BRITTANY EXPRESS

UNLIKE many south-western boat trains (see p27), this one did not run as an as-required 'Q train', but on a regular basis, running from Waterloo to Southampton Docks on Mondays, Wednesdays and Fridays, and northbound on Wed/Fri/Sun. It connected with St Malo steamer services and was in operation from 1954 to 1964 (sailings to St Malo having ceased in the autumn of 1963).

THE BROADSMAN

SO widespread were titled trains on the UK railway network at one time that even the relatively small Norfolk resorts of Cromer and Sheringham warranted one.

Today, of course, Sheringham is an important name on the heritage railway map, but in the early years of the British Railways era it was merely a seaside town on the single-track ex-Midland & Great Northern Railway system. The fledgling Eastern Region of BR had already tested the water there in 1948 by arranging for 'The Norfolkman' to pick up a summer-only Sheringham portion at Cromer Junction before continuing to Norwich and London.

Two years later, Sheringham became part of the itinerary of a new express, 'The Broadsman', which took its name from the large expanses of water that cover much of north-east Norfolk and which was launched onto the scene on June 5, 1950.

Departure time for the Sheringham coaches was 6.03am but, the following year, encouraged by the tremendous timetable accelerations made possible by the new 'Britannia' Pacifics, BR allowed Sheringham residents an extra quarter of an hour in bed by altering the time to 6.20, with arrival in London Liverpool Street at 10.07am. The northbound service left the capital at 3.30pm and the Sheringham coaches arrived at their destination at five past seven.

But there were even more accelerations to come a year later when 'The Broadsman' made headlines by

becoming the first regular mile-a-minute train in East Anglia and was once even timed at 94mph near Diss in 1954. For one timetable season, the Ipswich-Norwich leg was the fastest booked time in the UK.

Closure of Cromer High station in September of that year saw the train diverted into Cromer Beach, resulting in the Sheringham portion being joined and detached there instead of at the junction.

The English Electric Type 4s began to take over the service in the late-1950s, but on June 16, 1962, the Eastern Region withdrew the train, along with 'The Norfolkman' and 'The East Anglian'.

It was briefly resurrected in the Privatisation era of the late 1990s to describe the 6.55am Norwich-Liverpool Street and 6pm return.

THE BRUNEL (EXECUTIVE)

A TRAIN called 'The Brunel' appeared in the British Rail timetable of summer 1984/85, running as the 08.05 Paddington-Bristol Temple Meads and 16.40 return HSTs. By the summer of 1986, the title had been lengthened to 'The Brunel Executive' and applied to the 07.46 Bristol-Paddington. By May 1987, the name had ceased to be used on a regular basis but continued intermittently until 1993.

'BRUSSELS BOAT TRAIN'

CONNECTING with ferry services to the Belgian capital city and incorporating a Pullman bar, this service was introduced between London Victoria and Dover Marine by the Southern Railway in 1946 and continued by BR Southern Region from 1948 until its demise in 1954. It was an unofficial title, sometimes coming under the umbrella term 'Continental Express'.

'CAMBRIDGE BUFFET EXPRESS'

UNTIL the 1930s, the accepted route between Cambridge and London was via the former Great Eastern Railway route

CALAIS BOAT EXPRESS

A CHARING Cross-Folkestone service introduced by the South Eastern Railway in 1914.

Left: With steam to spare, 'Princess Coronation' Pacific No. 46224 *Princess Alexandra* is impatient to get 'The Caledonian' away from its Crewe call in pre-electrification days.

Below: In the early 1960s, it was common practice for the same headboards to be fixed to both steam and diesel locomotives. English Electric Type 4 No. D342 has the down 'Caledonian' near Hartford in May 1963. RAIL PHOTOPRINTS

Almost as illustrious as its famous LMS predecessor

SO well known is this prestigious West Coast express that many people assume it to have been introduced by the LMS, but in fact it was a product of British Railways' London Midland and Scottish Regions and didn't come into existence until the summer of 1957.

The LMS's famous 'Coronation Scot' streamliner was one of the victims of the Second World War – withdrawn at the outbreak of hostilities in 1939 and never reinstated. It was this glaring omission from the Euston timetable that the LMR officials tried to plug with 'The Caledonian', although of course, the fact that the streamlined 'Princess Coronation' Pacifics had all had their air-smoothed casings removed long before 1957 meant that this was never going to be a like-for-like replacement.

The train made its maiden run on June 17, 1957 – just 18 days short of the 20th anniversary of the inauguration of the 'Coronation Scot' – and, as with its illustrious predecessor, called only at Carlisle. But the departure times (8.30am from Glasgow and 4.15pm from London) were different and owed more to an East Coast express – 'The Talisman' – that had been launched the year before and was proving popular. From June 9, 1958, the West Coast authorities once again took a lead from their colleagues on the Eastern, North Eastern and Scottish Regions and doubled the service with the addition of a 7.45am down and a 4pm up. The trains then became known as 'The Morning Caledonian' and 'The Afternoon Caledonian', although separate headboards are not thought to have been cast and 'Caledonian' headboards – which, incidentally, are considered by many enthusiasts to be have been the most aesthetically pleasing of the genre – continued to be carried by both trains.

The morning and afternoon services called at Stafford in addition to Carlisle but did not attract the expected clientele and were withdrawn the very same year, on September 12, 1958, making them some of the shortest-lived named trains of all.

By 1963, electrification work on the WCML was impacting heavily on schedules and in addition, 'The Caledonian' was now calling at places such as Wigan, Crewe and Stafford. Diesels had also started hauling the trains.

The abolition of this much-respected express came on September 4, 1964 – a year and a half before commencement of the Euston-Manchester/Liverpool electrified services.

The name was briefly revived in 1984 – but for a (northbound-only) service running between the Welsh and Scottish capitals of Cardiff and Edinburgh, which left Cardiff at 07.47 and split en route, its portions arriving in Glasgow at 15.15 and Edinburgh at 15.18. The southbound equivalent of that service was known as 'The Principality'.

The 'Caledonian' title was resurrected again, this time on its traditional Euston-Glasgow Central route, between 1993 and June 2002, and then yet again, briefly, for a Virgin Trains 'Pendolino' service in 2004.

As a 'footnote', the steam-age 'Caledonian' was one of several select titled trains in Britain to carry its name at the rear of the last coach as well as on the front of the locomotive.

Near journey's end: Having been detached from the main train en route, the four-coach Fort William portion of the 'Caledonian Sleeper' makes its way through the magnificent Highland scenery of Rannoch Moor behind Class 67 No. 67011 on June 12, 2009. RAIL PHOTOPRINTS

CALEDONIAN SLEEPER*

ALTHOUGH this could be construed as a brand name rather than a train name, the fact that there are only four trainsets as opposed to a large fleet and the fact that the service includes 'portions' in the finest traditions of titled trains, has justified its inclusion as a main entry in the survey rather than as a miscellaneous listing.

Not only that, but if this service were to be excluded on the grounds of being a 'brand name', then it could be argued that the fleet of 'Brighton Belle' EMUs should be excluded too (and that clearly would be preposterous!). To cap it all, the 'Caledonian Sleepers' are just about the only regular all-year-round everyday named trains still loco-hauled and, with up to 16 coaches at the London end, are the longest passenger trains on the UK's classic lines network.

The name 'Caledonian Sleeper' first appeared in British Rail publicity literature circa 1996, but, from 2004, began to be officially and fully applied to the ScotRail-operated overnight trains that run between London and Scotland.

There are two services, 'Lowland' and 'Highland', as staff know them, running Sundays to Fridays. The Lowland portion runs from London Euston to Glasgow, with a portion for Edinburgh that splits and joins at Carstairs.

The 'Highland' train – sometimes colloquially known as "The Deerstalker" – is a more complex operation and consists of three portions that run to and from Fort William, Inverness and Aberdeen – the portions joining and dividing at Edinburgh Waverley.

Between London, Carstairs, Edinburgh and Glasgow, the trains are currently hauled by Class 90 locomotives hired in from DB Schenker. The Inverness, Fort William and Aberdeen portions are hauled by locos from a dedicated fleet of DBS Class 67s fitted with cast-iron brake blocks. The Fort William portion is operated by an RTEB-fitted loco. The days when passengers would awake to the throaty sound of a Class 37 on the Highland section have now passed.

The 'Caledonian Sleepers' run six days a week, departing Euston at 21.15 for Aberdeen, Inverness and Fort William (20.55 Suns) and 23.40 for Edinburgh (22.30 Suns).

BRAND NAMES

THERE has been much confusion over the years between train names and brand names and it is hoped that this encyclopaedia will help make sense of what has become something of a minefield for historians.

A headboard… but for a brand, not a title.

There are exceptions to every rule – but, basically, a train title is one applied to a single pair of trains per day, regardless of whether one set of stock is used (out-and-back) or two (balancing turns). A brand name, on the other hand, tends to describe a service in which a number of trains run during the course of a day, all bearing the same title (e.g. 'Gatwick Express').

A lot of brands were run under the auspices of British Rail and were largely identified by window labels, but, in latter years, some have become the province of private operators. Some services featured dozens of trains a day, while others only operated a few 'crack' or 'select' named services on a route shared by otherwise ordinary trains.

It is easy to split hairs, but for the purposes of this directory, it has been decided to include most brands in the main directory – but to mark them as such, to differentiate them from individual named trains. The more generalised brand names, along with terms that were very sweeping such as InterCity 125, are listed below:

■ EUROCITY
■ EUROSTAR
■ EUROTUNNEL
■ INTERCITY 125
■ MOTORAIL
■ NETWORKER
■ NETWORK EXPRESS
■ TRANS-PENNINE

The term 'Trans-Pennine' (today also the name of a train operating company) has caused confusion over the years – by virtue of the fact that the title was carried on headboards' (pictured left).

An express by name... but not always by nature

IT is a common misconception that the title 'Express' suggested high speed. In most cases it did, but there were some delightful exceptions – at least for certain sections of a journey – and the 'Cambrian Coast Express' was a case in point.

When slogging up the 1-in-52 Talerddig incline in winter, the up 'CCE' could sometimes be down to 20mph or less and the fact that the winding line west of Welshpool was single-track through some of the most rustic countryside in the British Isles gave this famous train a certain 'cachet' that more conventional expresses couldn't hope to emulate.

The train's roots reached back to July 1921 when the GWR introduced a 9.50am restaurant car service from Paddington to Aberystwyth and Pwllheli. Over the next six years, the start time was altered several times and the Welsh-bound coaches even became a portion of another train for a while, but on July 15, 1927, the GWR finally gave Mid-Wales and its coastal resorts a permanent named train of their own, although it was summer Fridays and Saturdays only to begin with.

Between Paddington and Wolverhampton, where an engine change was made, the running was as brisk as that of any other GW express, but once the 'King', 'Castle' or other top-link loco had been replaced by a pair of 'Dukedog' 4-4-0s (or latterly a 'Manor'), the running became decidedly more relaxed – so much so that it took roughly six hours to reach Aberystwyth despite taking only two from London to Birmingham.

Withdrawn on September 9, 1939, as a result of the war, the named train was reinstated by BR on July 7, 1951 and three years later was expanded from a summer-only weekend service to a Mondays-to-Saturdays, year-round one. It continued until as late as March 4, 1967, by which time it had become the last ex-GWR train to carry a headboard.

The main train normally ran to and from Aberystwyth and was united with the Pwllheli portion at Dovey Junction, but for the last year of the train's existence, the Pwllheli section became a diesel multiple unit.

The demise of the 'CME' as a titled train came on March 4, 1967, the use on the main portion of 'Manors' (until 1965) and then Standard 4MT 4-6-0s, making it one of the last steam-hauled named trains to operate outside the Southern Region.

The name was half-heartedly perpetuated in the BR timetable between 1986 and 1991 for a service to Aberystwyth (extended to Pwllheli on Fridays-only for the first year), but by then the London terminus had been switched from Paddington to Euston and the route south of Wolverhampton thus changed accordingly.

A delightful scene as a little girl poses by 'Castle' 4-6-0 No. 7013 *Bristol Castle* at Shrewsbury as it waits to take over the London-bound leg of the 'Cambrian Coast Express' in 1962. JOHN CHALCRAFT

Steam remained on the Cambrian until the mid-1960s and Standard 4MT No. 75033 was one of the last locos left in service on the 'CCE'. GAVIN MORRISON

to Liverpool Street, but the LNER, which by that time had absorbed the GER, realised that overcrowding on the line could be eased if some of the services could be directed along the slightly longer ex-Great Northern Railway route from King's Cross via Hitchin.

The fact that the trains could be made to call at the then-new garden cities of Welwyn and Letchworth gave the LNER a marketing opportunity and, in May 1932, an all-new buffet car service was duly launched with the somewhat verbose title of 'Garden Cities and Cambridge Buffet Express' on its roofboards.

Departures from the capital ranged from 9.30 in the morning to 11.40 at night and the later services thus became popular with Cambridge University students, who came to refer to them as "Beer Trains". It seems that BR wanted a snappier name too, for when the trains reappeared in the timetable in 1948, the 'Garden Cities' part had disappeared.

In steam days, a variety of locos handled the services, but in the 1960s they settled down to Brush Type 2 haulage and then Brush Type 4s (Class 47s).

The title was officially dropped in May 1964, but the

Right: With a full rake of matching Western Region coaches in tow, 'Britannia' Pacific No. 70023 *Venus* bowls along with the 'Capitals United Express' shortly after the train was named to commemorate Cardiff's elevation to Welsh capital city status in 1955.
COLOUR-RAIL

trains continued to run and the buffet cars continued to be included in the formation until the implementation of the GN electrification scheme in February 1978. The last train ran on February 5, hauled by Class 47 No. 47100 and appropriately carried a Cambridge University Railway Club headboard.

CAMPBELTOWN BOAT EXPRESS
A GLASGOW & South Western Railway service from Glasgow to Fairlie Pier and Largs for connection with ferries to Campbeltown.

CAPITAL COAST EXPRESS
AN EMU service between London Victoria and Brighton during the last few years of British Rail operation on that route (1993-96). It ran three times a day and thus was neither a proper 'titled train' (as those tend to run only once a day in each direction) nor a 'brand' (a description that tends to embrace an entire service running throughout the day).

Introduced in October 1993, it ran to a clockface timetable, leaving Victoria at six (later eight) minutes past the hours of 10, 13 and 15 (Monday-Friday) and taking just 51 minutes to complete the journey, including a stop at East Croydon. The up trains departed at 50 minutes past the hours of 9, 11 and 14, although times did vary. In

1997, the service was renamed 'Connex Express' by the incoming franchisee.

CAPITAL ENTERPRISE
A BR Regional Railways name for the 06.55 Edinburgh-Stranraer Harbour and 18.47 return in 1990/91. This 'Super Sprinter'-formed service, which provided connections at Stranraer for the Larne ferry, was also sometimes known as 'The Capitals Enterprise'.

THE CAPITALS LIMITED
THANKS to Nigel Gresley's corridor tenders, the pre-war 'Flying Scotsman' had been a non-stop train during the summer months, but, in 1949, British Railways decided that the famous train should once again have intermediate calling points and that its summers-only relief train should become the 'non-stop' instead. Thus was born 'The Capitals Limited', so called because it linked the capital cities of England and Scotland. The inaugural 9.30am departure from King's Cross was conducted in a blaze of publicity on May 23, 1949, due to the unveiling of the headboard by film star Anne Crawford and the up train got under way from Edinburgh Waverley just a quarter of an hour later.

The trains were heavy ones, containing not only a kitchen car, a buffet car and two dining cars but, with something approaching pre-war opulence, a ladies' retiring room was also provided.

The train ran under this name until the end of the 1952 summer on September 13 before being renamed 'The Elizabethan' for the start of the 1953 season.

CAPITALS UNITED EXPRESS *
ALTHOUGH it had long been the principality's largest city, Cardiff did not formally become the capital of Wales until December 20, 1955. To commemorate the event, BR's Western Region created a new train name, bestowing the title 'Capitals United Express' upon the 8am Cardiff-London and 3.55pm return, with through coaches to and from West Wales.

The date of the event explains why the date of the train naming, February 6, 1956, occurred later than many other WR namings and why it occurred in the middle of

Below: Wearing experimental blue BR livery, A4 No. 60033 *Seagull* waits at King's Cross with The 'Capitals Limited' to Edinburgh.
COLOUR-RAIL

the winter timetable, rather than at the end of it.

The express lasted until June 12, 1965, but although it is long gone, the name 'Capitals United' was revived in May 2010 by First Great Western and is today used to identify the 05.58 Swansea-Paddington and 16.45 return HST service.

'CARDIFF PULLMAN'

In 1961, 'The South Wales Pullman' was changed from steam-hauled express to 'Blue Pullman' diesel unit and began running twice a day between Swansea and London.

Three years later, BR decided to add an additional return leg to prevent the special DMU lying idle during the middle of the day and it was that extra service that took the name 'Cardiff Pullman', albeit unofficially... in the timetables and on the roller blinds of the diesel units, the title 'South Wales Pullman' was retained.

The service left Paddington at 11am each weekday, arrived in the Welsh capital 2hrs 20min later having called at Newport, and was back in London at 4.50. In subsequent years, its timings underwent various speed-ups.

The Cardiff sobriquet is understood to have fallen out of use by 1969 and all 'Blue Pullman' diagrams ended with withdrawal of the fleet four years later.

CARMARTHEN BAY EXPRESS

A GREAT Western Railway service that ran between London Paddington and Tenby in the 1920s.

(THE) CAR SLEEPER LIMITED

INAUGURATED on June 15, 1955, this was the first of several innovative services that enabled passengers to travel with their motor cars – a concept that later became known as 'Motorail'.

Operating in summer only, it conveyed a mixture of car-carrying vehicles and passenger accommodation and, for its first three years, left King's Cross yard at 7.45pm with an arrival in Perth at 5.30am, every night except Fridays. The respective times for the up service were 8pm and 6.15am. For the first year of operation, it ran twice weekly, down on Sundays and Wednesdays, and up on Tuesdays and Saturdays. After that, it ran every night except Fridays.

The car-carrying concept was a British invention that later spread to continental Europe with great success, although it has since largely been abandoned in the country of its birth. The idea germinated in the Eastern Region of BR, whose officials thought it would be a good idea to let motorists travel from London to Perth by couchette and then be able to continue into the Highlands using their own transport.

The cars were at first loaded in a former goods bay to the west of King's Cross station but this part of the operation later switched to Holloway, a mile north of the terminus.

So successful was the idea that the couchettes soon gave

way to full sleeping car accommodation and the converted vans in which the cars were contained were replaced by purpose-built vehicles.

Soon, the other Regions of BR followed suit and, by the late-1950s/early-60s, car-carrier terminals had started to spring up all over the country. Even the relatively small Southern Region got in on the act with a Surbiton-Okehampton service. On the East Coast route, the Car Sleeper Limited was joined in 1960 by the 'Anglo-Scottish Car Carrier' (see p11).

Eventually, the London end of the operation was centred on Kensington Olympia and, in 1966, the service was standardised under the collective name 'Motorail'.

(THE) CATHEDRALS EXPRESS *

CATHEDRAL cities have always held a certain allure for travellers and the Western Region of BR was well endowed with such ecclesiastical locations. In 1957, it was decided to capitalise on the fact that the 4.45pm from Paddington served four of them – London, Oxford, Worcester and Hereford.

Carrying a headboard adorned by a three-dimensional representation of a bishop's mitre and featuring classical mediaeval-style script, the newly-christened service first ran on September 16, 1957 with the up train of the same name leaving Hereford at 7.45 each morning.

The service was an example of how the term 'express' was sometimes applied slightly inappropriately, for the train was at best a semi-fast, especially between Worcester and Hereford, and during some years of its existence, called additionally at places such as Evesham, Moreton-in-Marsh and Kingham.

It lasted as a named train until June 12, 1965, by which time the Western Region was virtually entirely dieselised. Brush Type 4s took over the service that year, but it is not known if any of them ever carried the elaborate headboard (although for the last day of Class 50 haulage on the Cotswold Line, May 15, 1982,

Right: 'Castle' 4-6-0 No. 7011 *Banbury Castle* at Paddington with the up 'Cathedrals Express' from Hereford. R C RILEY

Above: The 'Channel Islands Boat Train' was remarkable in that it ran along the streets of Weymouth. In this scene on the harbour tramway, a BRCW 'Crompton' Type 3 is gingerly easing past the parked cars that made the running of this train such a headache for the authorities. The headboard is at variance with the train's official title, which featured the suffix 'Express'.

such a board was ceremoniously fixed to the front of the loco for part of the final run).

In 1984, the name was revived by BR and it is still in use in 2012, describing First Great Western's 06.43 Hereford-Paddington and 18.22 return (Mon-Fri).

■ The LNER is also reputed to have run a train linking its cathedral cities – Norwich, Ely, Peterborough, Lincoln and York – but there is no evidence that it ever carried a name.

CENTENARY EXPLORER

A DIESEL loco-hauled service introduced between Glasgow Queen Street (Low Level) and Fort William in 1994 to mark the centenary of Fort William station. It ran for that year only.

CENTENARY EXPRESS

A EUSTON-Birmingham New Street service run by the London Midland & Scottish Railway in 1938 only, to mark the centenary of the London & Birmingham Railway.

CHANNEL ISLANDS BOAT EXPRESS

THE GWR opened its Weymouth quay line in 1865 and ran regular trains from Paddington to connect with Channel Island ferries. From the winter 1959 timetable, the Southern Region of BR took over the workings and, despite difficulties caused by parked cars on the harbour section, continued to run them from Waterloo until 1988. In 1981/82, the train briefly ran with a 'Channel Islands Boat Train' headboard, although the wording in the timetable continued to use the term 'Express'. Another variant known to have existed was 'Channel Island and Normandy Boat Ferry'.

In the early to mid 1990s, an electric multiple unit service entitled 'Channel Island Express' was operated from Waterloo to Weymouth, but the title was restricted to a timetable entry and to some station display screens.

CHESTER PULLMAN

A BRITISH Rail era service that operated for the duration of the summer 1988 timetable and ran between Euston and Chester in the down direction only. It left London at 10.15.

CITY EXPRESS

A TRAIN that ran from London's Holborn Viaduct station to Ramsgate. Introduced by the London, Chatham & Dover Railway in July 1896, it departed at 5.10pm and called at St Paul's before running non-stop to Westgate-on-Sea, calling thence at Margate and Broadstairs. Over the years, the calling patterns and times were varied, although a slip portion was often dropped at Faversham.

In June 1905, the title was dropped by the South

A crowd turns out to cheer what was then the world's fastest train, the 'Cheltenham Flyer', as it shoots through Tilehurst behind No. 5000 *Launceston Castle* on September 14, 1931. SCIENCE & SOCIETY LIBRARY

'CHELTENHAM FLYER'

THIS was an unofficial name for the 'Cheltenham Spa Express' (see next entry), yet, curiously, it had its own headboard for a while. Rectangular in shape and bearing the words "Cheltenham Flyer. World's Fastest Train", it was carried on September 14, 1931 and on other occasions, but, five years later, a more conventional curved board began to be used. Despite those embellishments, the train continued to be referred to in timetables by its official title.

Its last run as a GWR-operated titled service was on September 9, 1939, six days after the outbreak of the Second World War.

CHELTENHAM SPA EXPRESS *

THE genteel Gloucestershire town of Cheltenham may seem an unlikely player in the annals of world railway history, but that's precisely what happened in the 1920s.

The key to the achievement was the superbly-engineered Great Western main line between London and Swindon, nicknamed 'Brunel's Billiard Table'. So conducive was this 77-mile section to high-speed running that the GWR realised it had a chance of claiming the 'blue riband' of railway speed, which at that time was held by the LNER, courtesy of the York-Darlington 'racing stretch'.

On July 9, 1923, the GWR had inaugurated the 'Cheltenham Spa Express' and it was this train that was chosen for a dramatic speeding-up, so much so that by 1929 it had become the fastest regular railway run in the whole world, earning it the nickname 'The Cheltenham Flyer' (see left).

This feat prompted the GWR to fit a special headboard proclaiming 'World's Fastest Train'.

Illustrating just how incredibly far railways have advanced since then, the average speed was only just over 66mph, but after briefly losing the world title to the Canadian Pacific Railway, the GWR gradually speeded the 'Flyer' up again until, in September 1932, it was completing the run in 65 minutes for an average of 71.4mph.

That year was also noted for an astonishing one-off

Eastern & Chatham Railway (which had succeeded the LCDR in 1899), but it was revived as a descriptive term in July 1921 when a number of 'City Express' entries appeared in the timetables to describe various London-Ramsgate fast services until July 1927, when the term was finally dropped.

THE CITY LIMITED

THIS was a quasi-official name for the London, Brighton & South Coast Railway's 8.30am service from Brighton to London Bridge and 4.45pm return.

Introduced in 1921 and composed mainly of first class stock with several Pullman vehicles, it grew in length and importance over the decades to become one of the heaviest trains in the south of England – yet despite that status, the LBSCR is thought never to have formalised the name by which its staff and patrons referred to it. Even the LBSC's successor, the Southern Railway, mentioned it only on the pages of its timetable and even that reference was dropped upon the outbreak of the Second World War.

The train was important enough to warrant purpose-built 12-car electric multiple unit stock when the switch was made from steam operation on January 1, 1933, but with numerous changes to departure and arrival times over the years, the name gradually faded from general use even among employees and regular passengers.

CITY-TO-CITY EXPRESS

MANY have been the inducements laid on by railway companies to attract custom. Hairdressing salons on the LNER streamliners of the 1930s is a facility often quoted, but the old London & North Western Railway had been displaying innovation as far back as 1910.

In that year, it laid on an experimental service to take commuters from Birmingham into the heart of the City of

L & N.W.R. City to City Express Birmingham to Broad Street.

London instead of to Euston (hence 'City to City Express'). The terminus was the ex-North London Railway's Broad Street – and to tempt businessmen to make the switch, the LNWR provided a typewriting compartment, complete with typist!

In a precursor to today's laptop and wi-fi age, it was thought that businessmen would appreciate the opportunity to get a bit of work done on the way in. But old habits die hard and insufficient numbers of businessmen were tempted. Perhaps the relatively late timings had a lot to do with it – the 2¼-hour train didn't reach Broad Street until 10.35.

The outbreak of World War One in 1914 gave the LNWR the excuse to withdraw the train and it never reappeared.

Above: A 1910 postcard image of the LNWR's Birmingham to London 'City-to-City Express', which used London's Broad Street terminus rather than Euston.

sprint by 'Castle' No. 5006 *Tregenna Castle* on June 6, 1932, which reeled off the journey in 56 minutes at an average speed of just under 82mph.

The accolade was lost in 1935 to the LNER's 'Silver Jubilee' and by rapidly-accelerating speeds elsewhere in the world, but Cheltenham had had its moment of glory.

A great irony, of course, is that the town itself was never part of the record-breaking achievements; it merely lent its name to them, for the section west of Swindon was not suitable for ultra high-speed running. Indeed, it was not unknown for the train to be worked over the section from Cheltenham St James to Gloucester Central by a tank engine!

At Gloucester, the six-coach train reversed direction, with the tank coming off and a 4-6-0 coupling onto the opposite end – a long-winded operation that in many respects defeated the object of the fireworks that were to come later. Before then, though, the 'Flyer's overall timings would have been increased still further by calls at Stroud and Kemble and a stiff climb to Sapperton tunnel.

The famous express failed to reappear in the GWR timetables after the war, but made a grand comeback under the auspices of BR on September 17, 1956, when the title was conferred upon the 8am up and 4.55pm down services and it continued to run until May 4, 1973, by which time track remodelling had negated the need for reversal.

The name was briefly revived in the BR timetable in 1984 and was then featured by the Great Western TOC during the early years of Privatisation. Today it is used by First Great Western to describe its 11.48 Paddington-Cheltenham and 14.31 return.

One of the best-known trains in the world – the 'Cheltenham Spa Express', at speed behind 'Castle' No. 7035 *Ogmore Castle* on June 18, 1962. HUGH BALLANTYNE

'CLACTON BELLE'

THIS was the Sunday version of the summer-only 'Eastern Belle' and was in operation between 1929 and 1939, running from Liverpool Street to Clacton, Essex. The name was informal but the train is included on account of it being a regular service in the LNER timetable, whereas the weekday 'Eastern Belle's main listing is in the holiday trains section (p57) because it ran to a different resort each day.

(CLACTON INTERVAL SERVICE)

(*Descriptive term*): This was the name of a regular service between London Liverpool Street and Clacton (including a portion for Walton-on-the-Naze). In the days when the train was loco-hauled, the name was carried for a while on carriage roofboards.

(THE) CLACTON PULLMAN

THE predecessor of the 'Eastern Belle', this GER/LNER Sunday service ran from 1922 to 1929 before its renaming. This was the title to which it was always referred by the LNER and the Pullman Car Company in their formal literature, although most railwaymen and members of the public called it the 'Clacton Belle' (see above). In 1928, the train went by the name of the 'Clacton Sunday Pullman'.

THE CLANSMAN

THIS name was coined during the Inter-City 'Electric Scots' era to identify a through day train from London Euston to Inverness via the West Midlands.

'The Clansman' made its inaugural run in 1974 just after completion of the full-length London-Glasgow electrification scheme, and was almost certainly the first named train to call at the new Birmingham International station when that opened two years later.

The train had a marathon all-day journey of almost 11 hours, not arriving in the Highland capital of Inverness until late evening (times varied over the years). Its timing was not helped by the need to change from electric to diesel traction – an operation carried out in Mossend marshalling yard between the station calls of Motherwell and Stirling. In 1985, the train included a Saturdays-only portion that had worked through from Paignton, Devon. In later years, 'The Clansman' ran only to Edinburgh but, in 1989/90, included an Aberdeen portion.

CLEVELAND EXECUTIVE

A BUSINESSMEN'S express from Middlesbrough to London King's Cross, introduced in January 1981.

Taking its name from a north-eastern county that existed between 1974 and 1996, the 'Cleveland Executive' initially departed Middlesbrough at 07.08, calling at Eaglescliffe, Northallerton and York, and arrived in London just over three hours later. The return working left King's Cross at 16.40.

From May 1983, the times were revised to enable the Class 254 HST operating the service to start and finish its journey at Newcastle, allowing the communities of Stockton, Hartlepool and Sunderland to benefit from a fast direct service to the capital too. By October 1989, the train ran in the up direction only and by May 1990 had been discontinued.

CLIFTONVILLE EXPRESS

A SERVICE run by the London, Chatham & Dover Railway from London's Holborn Viaduct (and Victoria) station to Ramsgate Harbour, but only in the summer of 1894 and only in the down direction.

The title was reintroduced by the South Eastern & Chatham Railway in October 1911 to describe a 9.10am London Victoria to Ramsgate Harbour train and a 5pm return. The title of the down service was dropped in January 1915 and the up train similarly became anonymous in the November of that year.

The titled trains were revived in July 1921 and ran, with numerous timing and calling amendments, until July 9, 1927 when the title was dropped, although the service continued to run. Cliftonville is a district in east Kent.

'THE CLUB TRAIN'

ALTHOUGH 'club trains' became popular with regular businessmen in the North-West of England in the 20th century (see left), there had been, between June 1889 and September 1893, two supplementary fare services bearing this word as a name, rather than as a description, running between London and Dover on the SER and LCDR in connection with cross-Channel sailings to/from Calais.

They were equipped not with Pullman cars but with saloon carriages purpose-built by the Wagons-Lits company to the British loading gauge, and bearing French wording – 'Voiture Salon' – on their bodysides.

THE CLYDESIDER

A BR Scottish Region Class 158 DMU service that ran between Aberdeen, Perth and Glasgow in the half-decade preceding Privatisation (1991 to 1996).

COAST LINE EXPRESS

A service run along the South Coast from Brighton to Salisbury, introduced by the London, Brighton & South Coast Railway in 1912.

THE COMET

NAMED not after a shooting star, but as a contraction of 'Cottonopolis' and 'Metropolis', 'The Comet' was launched into the railway universe on September 12, 1932.

'Cottonopolis' was a nickname for Manchester in the heyday of the hosiery industry, while metropolis, of course, refers to any huge conurbation, in this case London.

In its early years, the train departed from Euston at 11.50am, travelling via Stoke-on-Trent, and left Manchester London Road (now Piccadilly) at 5.40pm, running via Crewe. In the up direction, it was one of the fastest trains on the LMS and was so popular that, on Friday evenings, a fast relief was run ahead of it, thereby getting passengers to their destination a few minutes earlier.

In common with so many other named trains, it was withdrawn from the timetable on September 9, 1939, and reinstated almost exactly 10 years later, continuing until September 7, 1962. The main post-war change had been that the title of the northbound working was transferred to the 9.45am from London.

For many years, the train was synonymous with the 'Royal Scot' 4-6-0s until BR Standard 'Britannias' began to share some of the duties in the 1950s.

CONNEX EXPRESS

FORMERLY the 'Capital Coast Express', this fast service from London Victoria to Brighton was renamed by Connex South Central in 1997 after it took over the franchise from BR. It became a victim of Connex's demise and the name was dropped in May 1998.

 THE CONQUEROR
Tonbridge–Tunbridge Wells–Battle–
St Leonards(Warrior Square)–HASTINGS

THE CONQUEROR

NAMED after William the Conqueror and bearing the year '1066' on its window labels, this BR Southern Region electric multiple unit service ran as the 09.40 London Charing Cross-Hastings (fast) in 1986 to mark the introduction of electrified services along the route that year.

'THE CONTINENTAL'

ALTHOUGH most of the official named trains ending in the word 'Continental' were run to or from East Anglia (see 'Antwerp Continental', 'Day Continental' etc), the title "The Continental" (often shortened to "The Conti") has also been used informally by staff and locals over the years to describe almost any train that connects with steamer services on the south or east coasts.

Among them were a Birkenhead Woodside to Folkestone service, formed of a slip coach off a Birkenhead-Paddington train, and summer through coaches between Liverpool Central and Folkestone in 1899 (worked by Mersey Railway locos to/from Rock Ferry)

It is also understood that in the years leading up to the mid-1950s, a train used to run once a day in each direction along the Guildford-Reading line, carrying roofboards reading Birkenhead, Oxford, Margate and Dover.

Similar local terminology was used to describe a service on the London Victoria-Dover route (see below).

(CONTINENTAL BOAT EXPRESS)

(*Descriptive term*). This was a generic title used by the Southern Railway (and, before that, its constituents) to describe boat train services, such as those running from Victoria to Dover Marine. The name was often abbreviated to "The Conti" by staff and passengers.

CONTINENTAL EXPRESS

THE train of this name was a Great Eastern Railway service between Harwich Parkeston Quay and London Liverpool Street, introduced in 1864. It was withdrawn during the First World War but, by 1921, there were two a day in the timetable (6.30am and 7.48am from Harwich and referred to in some timetables as 'Continental Restaurant & Pullman Car Express'). Their balancing turns, at 8.30pm and 8.40pm in 1921, were named 'Hook of Holland Express' and 'Antwerp Express' respectively.

In the July 1938 Bradshaw's timetable, the plain term 'Continental Express' reappeared to describe a York to Harwich Parkeston Quay service. A footnote warned passengers: "This train will not be held if the Steamer is late".

The impressive orange headboard of the 'Oriana', seen on 'West Country' Pacific No. 34022 *Exmoor*. COLOUR-RAIL

SOUTH-WESTERN BOAT TRAINS

THERE were two distinct varieties of boat train. One type operated on a regular timetabled basis and mainly connected with ferries or packet steamers (such as those that ran to Harwich. Holyhead and Dover) while others ran specifically to meet ocean-going liners or long-distance cruise ships whenever they docked or left ports such as Southampton or Liverpool.

The former type are included in the main directory, but the latter are not as they ran on a purely 'as-required' basis in connection with the relevant international shipping lines. As dockings and departures of the transatlantic liners could be delayed by weather conditions at sea, the timings of such trains were at best unpredictable.

Many of the trains did, however, carry locomotive headboards, some of which were of similar style to those of regular named trains, and this has sometimes led to them being mistaken for the latter over the years.

To try to prevent such confusion, the following is an alphabetical list of the principal trains that ran under special traffic notices. Only those that ran on more than one occasion are included, as otherwise they would fall under the classification of one-off 'specials', which are not part of this survey:

- THE AROSA LINE
- THE CANADIAN PACIFIC
- CANBERRA
- THE CUNARDER *
- CUNARD SPECIAL
- CUNARD WHITE STAR
- EMPRESS VOYAGER *
- GREEK LINE
- HOLLAND-AMERICAN
- IMPERIAL AIRWAYS **
- THE NEWCASTLE VENTURER
- THE NORWAY CRUISE
- OCEAN MAIL/OCEAN LINER EXPRSS
- OCEAN TERMINAL EXPRESS
- ORIANA
- SITMAR LINE
- THE SOUTH AMERICAN
- THE SPRINGBOK
- STATESMAN
- SWEDISH LLOYD EXPRESS
- UNION-CASTLE EXPRESS
- UNION-CASTLE SAFMARINE

* 'The Cunarder' and 'Empress Voyager' names were also used in Scotland to identify Glasgow to Greenock Prince's Pier boat trains.
** These trains connected with flying boats.

THE CORNISHMAN *

THERE have been no fewer than seven entities where this train name was concerned, five official and two unofficial.

The first unofficial one is steeped in history, having started life in the broad gauge era of the Great Western and gaining immortality by becoming the last 7ft gauge train to leave Paddington for Cornwall on May 20, 1892.

This first 'Cornishman' came into being in June 1890 and soon established itself as one of the fastest trains in the country at the time. In spite of having to travel from

Penzance to Paddington via Bristol, a distance of 325 miles, and despite having to make a contractual stop at Swindon to enable passengers to use the private refreshment room there, it completed its journey in 8½ hours – around half of which was spent negotiating the Cornish and Devon banks.

In the early days of standard gauge operation on the GWR at the turn of the 20th century, the train became non-stop between London and Exeter, but the Great Western still didn't see fit to accord official sanction to the colloquialism and, after the 'Cornish Riviera Limited' had come into operation in 1906, the technically anonymous 'Cornishman' faded into obscurity.

The name (still unofficial) was revived on July 8, 1935 as a relief train to the 'Cornish Riviera', leaving Paddington at 10.35am and departing from St Erth on the up journey at 10.20am. It is not thought to have survived the war but, in June 1952, BR's Western Region resurrected it, and this time it was official.

The train on which the title was conferred was one that ran cross-country from Wolverhampton Low Level to Penzance via the 1908-built line through Stratford, Honeybourne and Cheltenham Malvern Road. Leaving Wolverhampton at 9.15am, it reached its destination at 5.55pm… not exactly express-like.

In the early-1960s, the usual 'Castle' class locos began to give way to diesel traction and, on September 10, 1962, the northern terminus was changed to Sheffield Midland. Three years later, the route was extended to Bradford Forster Square and then, on May 1, 1967, to Bradford Exchange, sending this somewhat glamorous train on a roundabout tour of relatively obscure South and West Yorkshire junctions.

In 1974, Leeds became the terminating point but 'The

Cornishman' was discontinued on May 3, 1975, only to appear for a fourth time in 1985/86 to describe an ultra long-distance Penzance to Edinburgh/Aberdeen working – which was soon renamed the 'Cornish Scot'.

(This recalled memories of an unnamed train known simply as the 'Aberdeen-Penzance service', which was jointly launched on October 3, 1921, by the North British, North Eastern, Great Central and Great Western companies and, at 785 miles, was the longest public journey in Great Britain. It was continued by the LNER and GWR but discontinued shortly after the war.)

'The Cornishman' title was used from winter 1987/88 to describe the 07.30 Penzance-Newcastle and the 11.25 in the opposite direction, which ran (with occasional Newquay, Glasgow and Dundee extensions) until 1998.

When Virgin CrossCountry took over from BR, it decided to revive the title and use it to identify the 702-mile Dundee-Penzance HST working (the 06.40 from Dundee and 09.22 return). The service was briefly described as 'The Cornish Connection', but this was never a formal title. As HSTs gave way to 'Voyagers', 'The Cornishman' name faded away once again, in June 2002.

However, that is not quite the end of the story, for, in December 2011, First Great Western created a seventh version of 'The Cornishman' when it resurrected the title to describe the 10.00 Penzance-Paddington and 15.06 return, thus bringing the story full circle 121 years after it started and giving this named train probably more variants than any other.

Penzance
Carstairs—Carlisle—Lancaster—Preston—Crewe—
Wolverhampton—Birmingham New Street—
Cheltenham Spa—Bristol Temple Meads—
Tiverton Parkway—Exeter—Plymouth—Liskeard—
Bodmin Parkway—Par—St. Austell—Truro—Redruth—
St. Erth

CORNISH SCOT

A TITLE devised by BR's CrossCountry sector in the 1980s to identify its Glasgow to Penzance service via Birmingham New Street.

At first, it was used to describe an Aberdeen/Glasgow to Plymouth/Penzance service in 1985/86, but, the following season, the name replaced that of 'The Cornishman' on the Edinburgh-Penzance itinerary.

The service was perpetuated for the first half decade of the Virgin CrossCountry era, but the introduction of 'Voyager' DEMUs brought about its demise and its last day of operation was June 2, 2002.

A train named by *Railway Magazine* readers

THANKS to a host of paintings, jigsaws and chocolate box covers, the 'Cornish Riviera' is probably the best-known named train after 'The Flying Scotsman' and 'The Royal Scot'.

In the 1930s and '50s, there can have been few people who did not set eyes at least once upon an image of it making its way past the idyllic, sun-kissed hillsides, beaches or cottages of Cornwall or Devon.

The Cornish Riviera was the nation's holiday train, the one that made children excited at the prospect of buckets and spades and copper-capped chimneys – and it also has a major connection with *The Railway Magazine*, for it was our readers who chose its name.

The history of this iconic service can be traced back to July 1904 when the GWR accelerated its main Paddington-Penzance service to reach its destination in seven hours, including what was then a world record non-stop run of 245 miles to Plymouth via Bath. Capitalising on public interest raised by this remarkable new schedule, the GWR and *The Railway Magazine* organised an exclusive competition in July 1904 to find a name for the train. More than 1,900 readers responded and the GWR chose 'The Riviera Express' as the winning title.

The two men who suggested it duly received prizes, yet when the naming took place two years later, the word 'Cornish' had been added and 'Express' had been changed to 'Limited' – words suggested by other readers who must have been upset that they too did not receive a prize!

Departure from Paddington was 10.30am (a time that was to remain constant until well into the BR diesel era) and the Plymouth section had been shortened by 20 miles thanks to the opening of the Westbury route.

To start with, coaches were slipped by the non-stop express at Westbury, Taunton and Exeter, but as the train grew in length and importance, it began to be divided into even more portions, including ones for Weymouth, Kingsbridge, Plymouth, Newquay, Falmouth and St Ives. Not all of those were slips, most being detached at station stops. For a while, the main portion terminated at St Ives.

By the end of the 1930s, it contained on some days nine different portions – as many as the 'Atlantic Coast Express' – and sometimes loaded to 15 coaches east of Westbury... a weight as great as 530 tons gross.

"The Limited" (as it was known by staff and regular patrons), had been withdrawn for a while during the First World War, from January 1, 1917 to July 6, 1919, but there

Above: The 'Cornish Riviera Express' makes a splash as its loco's tender is replenished from water troughs. COLOUR-RAIL

Left: The very last down loco-hauled 'Cornish Riviera Express' was powered by Class 50 No. 50009 on May 11, 1980. RAIL PHOTOPRINTS

is some confusion over what happened during the Second World War. In common with almost every other named train in the country, it was withdrawn officially on September 9, 1939, and wasn't formally reinstated until May 6, 1946 (although there is reliable evidence that it continued to run with its coach roofboards during the war).

British Railways continued the traditional title into the 1950s, but it is interesting to note that a one-off commemorative headboard cast for the train's golden jubilee in 1954 contained the name 'Cornish Riviera Express'. That must have been a harbinger because, four years later, the title was formally changed to match.

The 'Cornish Riviera Express' began running with that headboard in April 1958, by which time the first diesel-hydraulics were beginning to enter service on the Western Region, replacing the 'King' 4-6-0s that had in latter years made the train their own as far as Plymouth. In 1963, the 'Warships' began to give way to the 2,700hp 'Westerns' and a general speed-up of 'Riviera' times resulted.

Class 47s and Class 50s followed as air-conditioned stock replaced the BR Mk1 coaches and the time-honoured departure time from Paddington began to see changes, but the great InterCity 125 revolution was on the way and in the autumn of 1979, the "Limited" became an HST working. Schedules were accelerated substantially, departure times were changed again and the only clues to passengers that they were riding one of the all-time classic trains were paper stickers on the windows.

Nevertheless, the train clung tenaciously to its title, which (as 'The Cornish Riviera') is still in use today to describe First Great Western's 08.44 Penzance-Paddington (08.45 Sats) and 10.06 Paddington-Penzance.

Left: A quick final polish for the 'Cornish Riviera Limited' headboard on the first day of the summer 1956 timetable. *RM* ARCHIVE

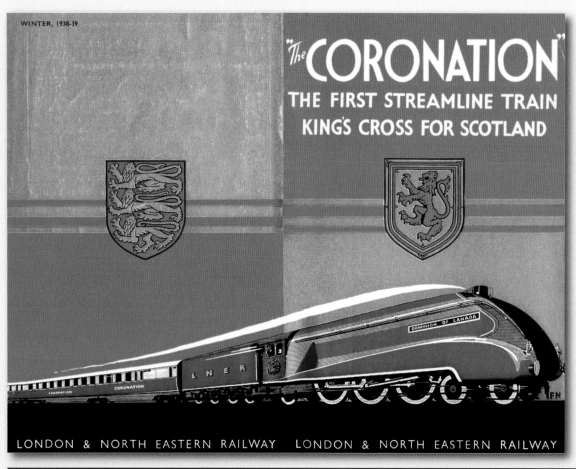

WINTER, 1938-39

"The CORONATION"
THE FIRST STREAMLINE TRAIN
KING'S CROSS FOR SCOTLAND

LONDON & NORTH EASTERN RAILWAY   LONDON & NORTH EASTERN RAILWAY

Left: A publicity brochure produced by the LNER for 'The Coronation' in 1938. The 'first streamline train' referred to the fact that it was the first to Scotland, the earlier 'Silver Jubilee' running only as far north as Newcastle. ROBERT FORSYTHE COLLECTION

Foot of page, left: Colour photography was in its infancy when the train was launched, so railway companies employed artists to create scenes such as this one on the Royal Border Bridge at Berwick-upon-Tweed.

Foot of page, right: One of the popular 'beavertail' observation coaches coupled at the back of the train. Note the name of the train on the rear-end.

THE CORONATION

THIS was the second of the LNER's glamorous 1930s streamliners and one of the most prestigious expresses in UK railway history – yet it was also one of the shortest-lived.

Introduced on July 5, 1937, on the back of the astonishing success of the 'Silver Jubilee', it was named in honour of that year's coronation of King George VI. However, whereas the 'Silver Jubilee' had been a relatively lightweight train, the new express was more than 40% heavier.

Like its predecessor, it had articulated carriages and featured an early form of air-conditioning called pressure ventilation. In summer only, a 'beavertail' observation car was attached to the rear, requiring to be turned at the end of each journey.

Unlike the silver-liveried coaches of the 'Jubilee', the new train sported a two-tone blue colour scheme to match a batch of five garter blue A4 Pacifics provided to haul it (Nos. 4488-to-4492, all named after nations of the British Empire).

Travel from Edinburgh to London and back on the same service in one day was not possible as both 'Coronations' set off in the afternoon, the down train at 4pm and the correspondingn service half an hour later. The overall times were six hours exactly with one, later two, stops northbound and one southbound.

The train quickly established a reputation for speed and luxury and, even though passengers were charged a supplement, it soon became as popular as its streamlined predecessor, prompting the LNER to introduce a third streamliner ('The West Riding Limited').

Who knows where it might have led to, but it all ended abruptly with the outbreak of war and although some of the coaches were stored in Scotland's Ballater carriage shed for the duration of the hostilities, the period of austerity that followed held no place for such unashamed luxury. Although the coaches were found uses in other trains, the crack named expresses never reappeared.

In some respects, that's a good thing... for the memory of the silver streamliners is thus preserved for ever.

"THE CORONATION"
CROSSING THE ROYAL BORDER BRIDGE BERWICK-UPON-TWEED
IT'S QUICKER BY RAIL
FULL INFORMATION FROM ANY L·N·E·R OFFICE OR AGENCY

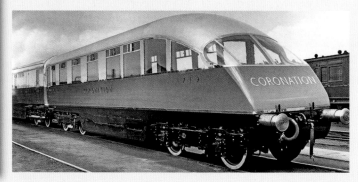

THE CORONATION SCOT

THERE has often been confusion, especially among the public, between 'The Coronation' and the 'Coronation Scot' and it is perhaps curious that – even in a coronation year – the LMS should deliberately have chosen a name so similar to that of its arch-rival, the LNER.

There are those who say the ploy caused unnecessary bewilderment for passengers and those who argue that it worked as a 'spoiler'. Whatever, there is no denying that both trains have gone down in history as wonderful successes and cemented the reputation of pre-war streamlined trains for all time.

The LMS may have been late getting in on the act where streamlining was concerned, but Stanier's air-smoothed 'Princess Coronation' Pacifics were as glamorous in their own right as the competitor company's Gresley A4s.

As with the LNER, 'The Coronation Scot' was launched to commemorate King George VI's crowning and made its

entry into traffic on July 5, 1937, following ultra-fast test runs in which the gauntlet was well and truly thrown down to Gresley and his Doncaster team.

The 'Coronation Scot' linked London Euston and Glasgow, weighed just under 300 tons and was turned out in a blue livery with thin white lines running the length of the locomotive as well as the train. In 1939, an all-new set of engines and coaches, painted in the same style but in maroon, made their appearance.

Start and finish times were exactly the same at both ends of the line – departure at 1.30pm and arrival at 8pm, and the privilege of riding on this most special of trains came at the expense of a supplement.

As with the LNER streamliners, the iconic 'Coronation Scot' was not resurrected after the war and the locomotives duly lost their streamlining.

The trains belonged to the art deco era of the 1930s... and died with it.

Above: An old Cumbrian shepherd and his dog take a moment to admire the awesome spectacle of the 'Coronation Scot' in full flight at Dillicar Common. The overall visual similarities between the crack trains of the LMS and LNER (facing page) can be appreciated in this juxtaposition. Painting by MALCOLM ROOT

Passing what is now the Olympic stadium site, B1 4-6-0 No. 61280 brings 'The Day Continental' through Stratford in 1956. The headboard featured the flags of the Netherlands and the United Kingdom.
COLOUR-RAIL

COTSWOLD & MALVERN EXPRESS

AN HST service introduced by British Rail on May 14, 1984, between London Paddington and Worcester, running through to Great Malvern. Within months, an increase of net revenue of 11.3% was reported over the DMU that had previously run in the same path.

In 1988, the train was extended to Hereford and renamed 'Cotswold Express'. It reverted to its longer title after just a year but was killed off in May 1997 after the incoming Great Western franchisee claimed that passengers were unaware that they were travelling in a named train.

CROMER EXPRESS

See 'Norfolk Coast Express'.

(CROSS COUNTRY EXPRESS)

(*Brand name*): A series of trains working variously between Edinburgh, Manchester and Birmingham New Street in 1995 and 1996 only, operated by British Rail's InterCity Cross-Country sector.

THE DAY CONTINENTAL

THE name by which the 'Flushing Continental' became known after the Second World War (see separate entry for earlier history). Its name had to be changed because the Zeeland Steamship Co had switched ports from Flushing to Hook of Holland. The word 'Day' referred simply to the fact that the train left Liverpool Street in mid-morning

and ran during the middle part of the day.

The first run took place in June 1947 and the service continued for almost exactly 40 years before being renamed 'The Admiral de Ruyter' by British Rail in May 1987.

One of the oddest chapters in 'The Day Continental's history occurred in the early-1950s when it was hauled for a short while by Bulleid Light Pacifics, the usual 'Britannias' having been taken out of service for safety checks.

In the latter years of the 'Day' and 'Hook Continentals', the restaurant cars were replaced by buffet cars.

DEESIDE EXPRESS

LIKE the Ballater Express, this Great North of Scotland Railway train linked Ballater with Aberdeen and was introduced in 1914.

"THE DEERSTALKER"

A NICKNAME for the Highland portion of the 'Caledonian Sleeper'.

THE DEVON EXPRESS *

VERY few all-new titles have been devised in recent years, but the First Great Western train operating company has given this name to its 07.06 London Paddington-Paignton service, which began running in May 2010. There is no corresponding named train in the opposite direction.

DEVON AND CORNWALL EXPRESS

A PADDINGTON to Falmouth train launched by the Great Western Railway in 1913 but withdrawn just a year later upon the onset of the First World War.

DEVON SCOT

A TITLE created by BR's Cross Country sector in May 1988 to identify its service from Aberdeen to Plymouth via Carlisle and Birmingham New Street – one of the longest journeys in the country.

When Virgin Trains won the Cross Country franchise in 1997, it perpetuated the operation for five years until the onset of VT's 'Operation Princess' resulted in all its train titles being discontinued in June 2002.

THE DEVONIAN

THIS was something of an oddity among titled trains, for its name was derived not from the main express (which terminated at Bristol) but from one of its through portions.

It was introduced as a Bradford-Paignton cross-country service and began running on September 26, 1927. The LMS operated the express from Bradford's Forster Square station down to Bristol Temple Meads, where the through coaches were handed over to the GWR for onward haulage. En route, the train had picked up a Newcastle-Bristol through coach and dropped off a Bradford-Bournemouth one.

The through Paignton and Kingswear coaches (usually three of them) warranted the carrying of a 'Devonian' headboard and, in BR steam days at least, it was carried west of Bristol too, although differences between LMS and GWR bracket fittings meant that the same one could not be used throughout.

Leaving Bradford mid-morning, the train served Leeds, Sheffield, Derby and Birmingham and got the citizens of those conurbations to south Devon by mid-

Easing into Bristol Temple Meads is 'Jubilee' No. 45690 *Leander* with 'The Devonian' in March 1962.
A JARVIS/COLOUR-RAIL

The 'Devon Belle' was unusual in having large wings on the smoke deflectors as well as a conventional headboard (but one featured the definate article and the other didnt!) 'West Country' Pacific No. 34011 *Tavistock* is shown sporting such embellishments at Exmouth Junction motive power depot in June 1949. COLOUR-RAIL

(THE) DEVON BELLE

ALTHOUGH Pullman cars had briefly been seen in Devon in 1880 on London & South Western metals and in 1929 on the Great Western Railway's short-lived 'Torquay Pullman', it wasn't until 1947 that the Southern Railway followed suit.

'The Devon Belle' made its maiden journey in June of that year and ran from London Waterloo to the resort of Ilfracombe, with a through portion for Plymouth Friary. The luxury train was a summer weekends-only service and was so popular that the main Ilfracombe section sometimes had to be strengthened to 10 coaches, making 14 in all – a tough call on the stiff West Country gradients. Fortunately, the SR's relatively new Pacifics made such operations possible, Class 8 'Merchant Navies' handling the full-length train as far as Exeter Central and Light Pacifics taking the two portions on to their respective destinations.

In addition to being banked up the 1-in-37 between Exeter St David's and Exeter Central, the London-bound Ilfracombe train had to tackle 2¼ miles of 1-in-36 immediately upon leaving the seaside resort, an exercise that often meant Pacifics at front and rear – an extra attraction for passengers fortunate enough to be sitting in the observation car at the rear of the train.

The observation cars – the only ones to run regularly on Southern metals – carried the words 'Devon Belle' on the rear and, for the last year of the train's existence, the definite article was dropped from the locomotive headboards to match.

On the subject of embellishments, this train sported some of the most notable – huge 'wings' attached to the side of the air-smoothed casings of the Bulleid Pacifics in the early-1950s.

After three seasons, the Plymouth portion was discontinued in 1949 and thereafter the journey time of the down train (but not the up) was a little shorter, the noon departure from London arriving in Ilfracombe at 5.27pm. Although the 'Belle' carried third-class passengers as well as first, the charging of a supplement combined with increasing car ownership was starting to have an effect and decreasing patronage caused the Southern Region to pull the plug, the final service operating on September 19, 1954.

Above: This stylised image of the observation car helped promote the train to the public in its first year, 1947.

A superb portrait of 'The Devon Belle' curving slowly across Barnstaple Bridge, with the River Taw below. At the head of the London-bound train is 'West Country' Pacific No. 34041 *Wilton*. Painting by MALCOLM ROOT

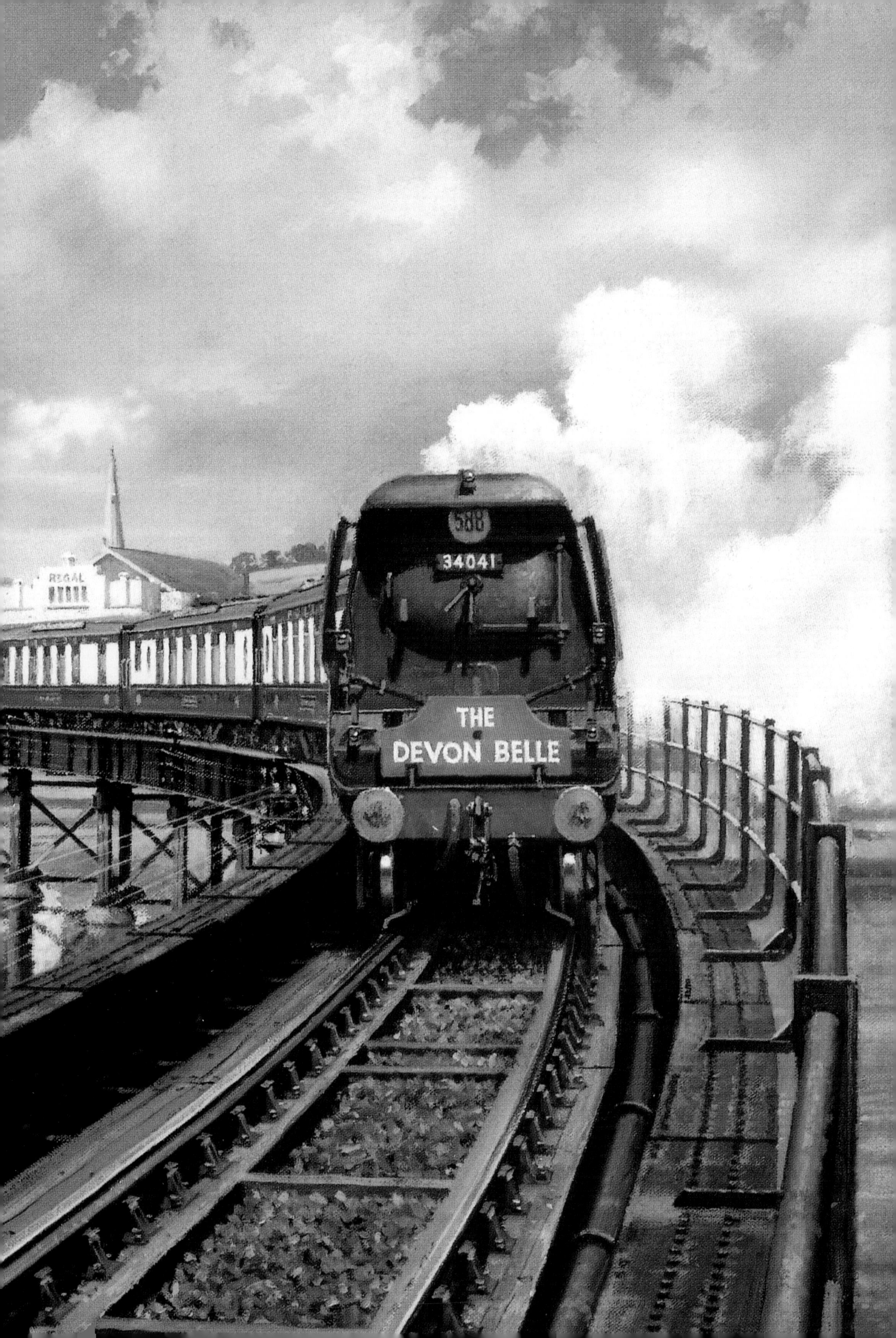

588
34041
REGAL
THE
DEVON BELLE

evening. In the opposite direction, the through coaches set out on their long journey at 9.15 and, in the early years at least, the train required banking up the Lickey incline.

In the mid-1960s the train's official destination was Dartmouth, but because that was not rail-connected, it ran only as far as Kingswear, from where passengers could catch a ferry. After BR closed the Kingswear line, the destination reverted to Paignton.

In May 1967, Bradford Exchange became the starting point and, four years later, it was changed again, this time to Leeds City. By then, diesel haulage had rendered the engine change at Bristol unnecessary and the train ran throughout, normally behind a 'Peak' class Type 4 and later as an HST-formed set.

The fact that numerous large cities were linked by 'The Devonian' probably accounted for the train's longevity, for, apart from a gap for the war, it lasted from 1927 until May 1975 and then reappeared in the national timetable as a Leeds-Paignton (later Newcastle-Paignton) service in 1987/88, moving from an 06.15 ex-Leeds time to 07.45 to make way for 'The Armada'.

By 1990, the summer 'Devonian' was departing Leeds for Paignton at 08.30, but although the title survived into the Virgin Trains era, it disappeared in the great purge of CrossCountry names in June 2002.

DORSET SCOT

A NAME devised in 1990 by BR's CrossCountry sector to identify its Edinburgh to Poole service via Newcastle, Birmingham and Reading. It was withdrawn in 1992 but reintroduced in 1994 and then perpetuated by Virgin CrossCountry.

DOVER PULLMAN EXPRESS

TWO trains with similar titles plied between London Victoria and Dover Pier in pre-war days. The 'Dover Pullman Car Boat Express' was operated by the London, Chatham & Dover Railway between 1882 and 1884 and the 'Dover Pullman Continental Express' was a Southern Railway service active from 1924 to 1929. The earlier of the two ran with only one Pullman car in the rake, whereas the later train comprised a full set. They sometimes appeared in the timetables under the generic term 'Continental Express'.

The Dubhlinn
BLACKPOOL NORTH
Bangor-Llandudno Junction-Colwyn Bay-Rhyl-Prestatyn-Chester-Warrington Bank Quay-Wigan North Western-Preston

REGIONA: RAILWAY

NW

NorthWest express

THE DUBHLINN

UNUSUAL in that it used an original form of spelling for the Irish capital city, this train ran from Blackpool North to Holyhead, from where passengers could catch ferries to Dublin. It was operated by the North Western Trains TOC between 1995 and 1997 and normally utilised a Class 156 'Sprinter' unit.

EASTBOURNE PULLMAN LIMITED

IN 1909, the London Brighton & South Coast Railway launched a steam-hauled Pullman car train leaving London Victoria at 10.45am and Eastbourne at 5.15pm,

THE EAST ANGLIAN *

Liverpool Street's most prestigious service

A rare shot of a streamlined B17 in British Railways livery. No. 61659 – appropriately named *East Anglian* – is bearing the identically-worded headboard in the locomotive-servicing yard at London Liverpool Street in August 1949. CLIVE FIELD

both journeys taking 90 minutes exactly.

There was also a Sunday equivalent called the 'Eastbourne Sunday Pullman Limited'. Known more generally, even by the LBSCR itself, as the 'Eastbourne Limited', the services continued intermittently until 1935, by which time they had come under Southern Railway jurisdiction.

EASTBOURNE SUNDAY LIMITED

See above entry.

EASTBOURNE PULLMAN

ON summer Sundays in the 1950s, British Railways Southern Region used a spare 'Brighton Belle' EMU set to run a service between Victoria and Eastbourne called 'The Eastbourne Pullman'. Its origins lay in a similarly-named steam-hauled train operated by the LBSCR and SR (see previous two entries).

The BR version of the train was inaugurated in 1950 and was fondly and informally referred to by its users and staff as the "Eastbourne Belle". It was withdrawn in 1957.

THE Great Eastern main line has long played second fiddle to the more glamorous East Coast route and that was never more so than in 1935 when the streamlined A4s and the 'Silver Jubilee' began to appear on the latter line. So when the LNER – which controlled both lines at the time – introduced 'The Coronation' between King's Cross and Edinburgh in 1937, it also gave the Liverpool Street division of its empire something to cheer too... its own streamlined train.

'The East Anglian' consisted of two six-car sets constructed in the manner of the East Coast stock with two B17 4-6-0s clad in A4 Pacific-style streamlining.

Unfortunately that's where the similarity with the Anglo-Scottish route ended, for it soon became clear that the air-smoothed casing was not going to be needed for anything other than cosmetic purposes; The new train would average less than 55mph on its journey to Norwich and back.

At least the LNER didn't have the effrontery to make a surcharge for the service, even when it improved the schedule the following year to almost a mile-a-minute – the fastest at that time on the Norwich line.

Service inside the sleek carriages was up to similar standard to the East Coast streamliners, though, and passengers were served freshly-cooked meals at their seats.

The 'East Anglian' was withdrawn on August 31, 1939 and (unlike the three East Coast streamliners) reinstated after the hiatus on October 7, 1946 – but it was difficult to re-create the pre-war glamour and in 1951 the two B17s lost their streamlined cladding.

That was the year 'Britannia' Pacifics began to appear on the ex-GE main line and

A happy renaissance for the title came in 1980 and Class 47 No. 47160 is seen at Liverpool Street on September 8 of that year. The headboard has gained the definite article and the emblems depict the arms of the cities of London and Norwich. HUGH BALLANTYNE

those brand new machines brought a much-needed fillip to what had been a 'Cinderella' line for too long. Seven years later, the Liverpool Street-Norwich trains became some of the first in the country to be handed over to Type 4 diesel power when English Electric Type 4s, again brand new, arrived on the scene.

Despite those advances, 'The East Anglian' was withdrawn as a titled service on June 16, 1962 – but it made a surprise reappearance 18 years later when the Eastern Region of British Rail decided to resurrect the name on May 12, 1980 for a London-Yarmouth train, in connection with a speeding-up of the timetable. The title was applied to the 8am from Norwich and the 4.20pm from London and

the old 2¼ hours was slashed to 110 minutes for the 115 miles.

The title survived into the Privatisation era and was used on the 07.55 from Norwich to the capital and the 17.00 return until 1998, when it was discontinued. It is understood that it was worked at least once by a preserved Class 55 'Deltic' (No. D9000) and also by Class 170 'Turbostars'.

In May 2011, the title was again officially reinstated, this time by National Express East Anglia to describe its flagship service on the London-Norwich route. Now under the control of the Greater Anglia franchise, the train remains in the 2012 timetable as the 07.40 from Norwich and the 17.00 return.

THE EASTERLING

IT is not certain how this train gained its name, except that it was introduced in 1950 – just a year after J R R Tolkein's 'Lord of the Rings' novel appeared containing the word.

As the train was one run by the Eastern Region and would serve Britain's most easterly town (Lowestoft), it seemed as logical a name as any.

'The Easterling' was a summer-only service linking London Liverpool Street with Lowestoft Central and Yarmouth South Town. Interestingly, the train was divided at Beccles on each journey and the portions for those two destinations were then rejoined at Beccles on the way back.

The inaugural journey ran on June 5, 1950 and the final one on September 6, 1958.

'EASTERN BELLE'

THIS unique LNER operation visited a different East Anglian resort each day of the week. For details, see Holiday Trains panel (p57) and also under 'Clacton Belle' and 'Clacton Pullman'.

Rarely photographed in colour was 'The Easterling'; the southbound working of which is seen behind a B17 4-6-0 on the Great Eastern main line in the 1950s. COLOUR-RAIL

On May 6, 1974, British Rail introduced a rare (and possibly unique?) example of a headboard bearing a plural title. 'The Electric Scots' board was fixed to West Coast electric No. 87024, seen en route from Glasgow Central to Euston. PATRICK RAWLINSON

EDINBURGH PULLMAN

THIS title was coined on July 13, 1925 when the 'Harrogate Pullman' was extended to Edinburgh Waverley and given the official name 'Harrogate and Edinburgh Pullman' – more commonly known as the 'Edinburgh Pullman'.

After two months, its Bradford portion was transferred to a new train, 'The West Riding Pullman', enabling the 'Edinburgh Pullman' to bypass Leeds and run non-stop between King's Cross and Harrogate via Church Fenton.

The train lost its identity on December 1, 1927 when it was officially renamed 'The Queen of Scots'.

In 1992, the name came back into use informally as a way of describing the Edinburgh version of 'The Scottish Pullman' (that official title having been given by British Rail InterCity to King's Cross trains that served both Edinburgh and Glasgow).

(THE ELECTRIC SCOTS)

(*Brand name*): A generic term coined by British Rail in the 1970s to describe any of its newly-electrified Anglo-Scottish express services from London Euston. It was not, therefore, a specific train but the name was extremely unusual for a plural term in that it was carried on a headboard (see picture, left).

THE EMERALD ISLE EXPRESS

PASSENGERS taking the 8.45pm 'Irish Mail' from Euston to Holyhead had to transfer from train to ship in the early hours of the morning, so wily customers were in the habit of taking the 5.15pm train and getting into their cabins on the steamer before midnight.

So popular did this train become that the London Midland Region decided it warranted a faster schedule and a name of its own. Thus was born 'The Emerald Isle Express' in September 1954.

The London departure time was improved to 5.35pm, followed by a non-stop run to Stafford with subsequent pick-up calls made at Crewe, Chester and Llandudno Junction. For the return, the name was bestowed upon the 7.30am from Holyhead. As a result of the upheaval caused

THE ELIZABETHAN

The world steam speed record holder, A4 No. 60022 *Mallard*, gets 'The Elizabethan' away from Edinburgh Waverley in September 1961. COLOUR-RAIL

A young spotter at York adds the number D9021 to his notebook as the new 'Deltic' heads for London with 'The Elizabethan' in June 1962. RAIL PHOTOPRINTS

IT is a measure of how long the present monarch has been on the throne when it's considered that 'The Elizabethan' train title had not even been coined when she came to the throne in 1952, yet is now a fondly-remembered (and fairly distant!) piece of railway history.

This famous express was not an all-new train when it appeared on the scene on June 29, 1953, but a re-naming of 'The Capitals Limited' in honour of Queen Elizabeth II, who had been crowned just a few days before the inaugural run of this summer-only train.

British Railways took the opportunity to speed up the timetable, from 7hrs 5mins to 6 ½ hrs to and from Edinburgh, making this 393-mile, 425-ton schedule (much of which had to be reeled off at an average of a mile-a-minute) an extremely challenging one and it was not surprising that it was entrusted only to a well-maintained A4 Pacific and a top-link crew.

From 1953/4 to the summer of 1961, inclusive, the non-stop train ran Mondays-to-Fridays only. (At weekends, there was an unnamed equivalent, using the same locos and stock but with the headboard reversed to show the blank side and running to a slower schedule).

The prestigious train, with its plush, pressure-ventilated stock was normally "Streak"-hauled until English Electric 'Deltics' took over from June 1962. Although they too were masters of the schedules, there was heavy irony insofar as their lack of a corridor brought an end to non-stop running between London and Edinburgh... as a call had to be made at Newcastle to change crews.

The 'Elizabethan' headboards continued to be carried by the diesels, but only for one season as the title was discontinued on September 7, 1962 and the train reverted to being a relief to 'The Flying Scotsman'.

by the West Coast electrification, the train was diverted in the early 1960s via the Birmingham loop line, stopping at Coventry to change from electric to diesel traction, but the temporary pain was worth the gain, for completion of the work saw the Euston departure time improved by almost an hour, to 6.35pm, despite continuation of the loop route for the down 'Emerald'. Oddly, the up version of the train used the more direct Trent Valley Line.

The train ceased to run as a titled express on May 3, 1975, but the port of Holyhead remains an important destination for trains and the title was resurrected by British Rail between 1993/4 and 1997 for a Birmingham International-Holyhead service.

ESBJERG CONTINENTAL EXPRESS
THE name by which the LNER boat train 'The Scandinavian' was known between 1928 and 1930.

THE ESSEX COAST EXPRESS
IN many instances, trains that had been quietly and anonymously going about their business for a great many years suddenly gained a name when a change of motive power brought about a substantial acceleration.

Such was the case with the 7.51am breakfast car train from Clacton-on-Sea to London Liverpool Street and the 5.27pm return, which (with varying start and finish times) had been in operation since Edwardian times, but which, in the twilight years of steam, officially became known as 'The Essex Coast Express'.

The title was deemed necessary after 'Britannia' Pacifics were cascaded from the main London-Norwich runs as a result of dieselisation. The first run in its new guise took place on June 9, 1958 when pioneer 'Brit' No. 70000 bore a huge circular headboard covering the whole of the smokebox door for maximum publicity. Subsequent trains carried more normal-sized embellishments.

The title, rather surprisingly, remained in use when the Essex commuter and holiday route was electrified – and again greatly accelerated – five years later. It wasn't formally discontinued until May 3, 1968, by which time it had been an electric multiple unit service for five years. None of the EMUs is thought to have carried the headboard.

As an interesting aside, the 'Essex Coast Express' was on at least once occasion in September 1958 hauled by a Scottish Region 'Clan' Pacific after No. 72009 *Clan Stewart was* temporarily borrowed by the Eastern Region for a short period of trials.

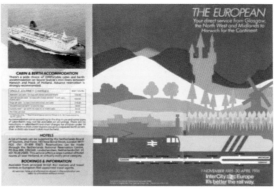

Sadly, titled trains were to most intents and purposes anonymous from the 1970s onwards, only small labels in the windows revealing their identity. This was 'The European', arriving at Carlisle behind Class 86 No. 86240 on September 18, 1986. The publicity brochure advertising the train is far less shy! Top picture: HUGH BALLANTYNE

THE ESSEX CONTINENTAL
A NAME used by British Rail between 1986 and 1988 for the 09.10 London Liverpool Street-Harwich Parkeston Quay and Harwich Town service.

(ESSEX EXPRESS)
(Brand name): A short-lived term coined by British Rail in the 1980s for a number of limited-stop EMU services serving London Liverpool Street.

EUROCITY EXPRESS
(Brand name). A general term given by British Rail to a number of services to and from Harwich Parkeston Quay in the 1980s.

EUROSTAR LINK. See page 41

THE EUROPEAN
THIS was one of several titles used over the years to describe boat trains connecting with Hook of Holland ferries at Harwich Parkeston Quay. It was introduced in 1983 to describe the 07.17 Harwich to Edinburgh and 11.06 southbound service, traversing the country via Manchester, Sheffield, Nottingham, Peterborough, Ely and Ipswich. A portion ran from Peterborough to Glasgow via Manchester and Bolton.

By summer 1986, the times had changed to 07.20 from Harwich and 10.15 from Edinburgh, but in September of that year, the train was re-routed to terminate at Manchester Piccadilly and renamed 'The Rhinelander'.
■ Circa 1984, BR had proposed altering the title of 'The European' to 'The European Scot'. New window labels were printed showing all 17 calling points from Glasgow Central (including Carstairs, Bolton, Grantham and March, but they are not thought to have ever been used.

THE EXECUTIVE
WHEN the West Coast Main Line timetable was being drastically speeded up as a result of electrification in the

Left of page: Large circular headboards were used frequently for one-off charters and works outings in the 1950s and 60s, but apart from the Southern Region, few areas of BR used them on regular trains. This one is thought to have been used only once, on the inaugural day of the 'Essex Coast Express', June 9, 1958, after which a conventional curved headboard was substituted. No. 70000 *Britannia waits* to leave Clacton. G R MORTIMER

So short-lived was 'The Fair Maid' that colour photos of it are scarce. This is A1 No. 60158 *Aberdonian* at Darlington station in August 1958. COLOUR-RAIL

1960s, BR realised that the commuter net could be cast still further from London and one of the towns to gain a fast breakfast train to London was Wolverhampton.

The up service left Wolverhampton at 7.22am and was in the capital by 9.21am, having called at Hampton-in-Arden and Coventry to pick up more 100mph long-distance commuters. The return train started from Euston at 5.45pm and, as with the breakfasts, a supplementary fare was necessary if a supper was required. It also covered the 126 miles in a minute short of two hours.

'The Executive' began in spring 1967 and disappeared as a named train in 1972.

(EXMOUTH EXPRESS)

(*Brand name*): A description for BR Cross Country trains serving Exmouth.

THE FAIR MAID

MOST named trains on the East Coast Main Line have had reasonably lengthy lives, but an exception was 'The Fair Maid', which, despite its attractive name, survived for only a year.

It took its title from a novel by Sir Walter Scott, The Fair Maid of Perth, and linked that city with London King's Cross.

The train was in actuality the 'Morning Talisman', which had been extended to Perth and renamed as an experiment. Its maiden run took place on September 16, 1957, but unfortunately, the experiment didn't prove a success and the final run was made on September 12, 1958, giving 'The Fair Maid' a rather less than fair lifespan of under a year.

For the following season, the name reverted to the 'Morning Talisman'.

THE FAST BELFAST

POSSIBLY the only train name whose words rhymed, the 'Fast Belfast' was an LMS service that ran over the ex-Glasgow & South Western Railway route from Glasgow to Stranraer to connect with steamers sailing for Larne, in Northern Ireland.

A summer-only restaurant car train, it began running in 1933 and left Glasgow St Enoch at 3.50pm to get its passengers to the ferry in time for a 10pm arrival in Belfast. For those travelling the other way, arrival time at St Enoch was 3.28pm, six hours after leaving the Ulster capital. The service did not survive the Second World War.

THE FESTIVAL EXPRESS

MOST 'festival' trains ran only for the duration of their related event and are therefore not included in the main directory,

THE FENMAN

TODAY, the small Norfolk resort of Hunstanton is but a memory on the railway map, but six decades ago it was considered by BR to be important enough to warrant its own direct buffet car service to London.

'The Fenman' was inaugurated on May 23, 1949 and left Hunstanton at 6.45am, running into King's Lynn, where it had to reverse in order to continue towards London.

Further stops for this most relaxed of 'expresses' followed at Ely (in order to change engines) and at Cambridge, where a through portion from Bury St Edmunds was attached, and the train eventually rolled into Liverpool Street at 10.03am.

The return journey was even slower, leaving London at 4.30pm and averaging just 33mph for the journey to Hunstanton, which was reached just before 8pm..

From 1953 onwards, the Eastern Region realised that these timings were not really

'The Fenman' was usually rostered to a B17 or B1 4-6-0. In this 1950s scene, B1 No. 61329 is doing the honours.

competitive with road transport (car ownership in East Anglia at the time was growing more rapidly than anywhere else in England) and the schedule was duly speeded up. The Bury portion was turned into a train in its own right but any minutes gained by that change were negated by the introduction of a March and Wisbech portion, attached and detached at Ely.

By 1960/61, diesels were in charge, usually Classes 31 or the new 37s, and the residents of

Hunstanton had lost their direct link – a DMU shuttle service to King's Lynn having to suffice for the few years before total closure of the branch on May 5, 1969.

'The Fenman' didn't even last that long, losing its title exactly a year earlier, but the name unexpectedly rose from the dead on October 1, 1984 when it was resurrected for a Class 47-hauled service along the Cambridge main line, surviving until 1987.

but 'The Festival Express' – which was named in connection with the Stoke-on-Trent Garden Festival in 1986 – was in regular service between Euston and the Potteries for the whole of that summer's London Midland Region timetable.
■ A similar train – the 'Festival Rose' – had run between Euston and Liverpool Lime Street two years earlier.

THE FFESTINIOG RANGER

THIS Sundays-only train appeared in the BR national timetable in summer 1994 and 1995 and ran between Chester and Blaenau Ffestiniog, via the Llandudno branch. In the first year, it left Chester at 09.00 and Llandudno at 10.45, returning from Blaenau at 17.07.

THE FIFE COAST EXPRESS

THIS North British Railway train has a claim to fame in that it is believed to be the first to have regularly carried a locomotive headboard. It also became notable after the withdrawal of the 'Silver Jubilee' in 1939, for five of the luxury coaches from that streamlined train were taken out of wartime storage in the late 1940s and quietly put to work on this rather humdrum service.

'The Fife Coast Express' was introduced in 1911 and grew out of the 'Fifeshire Coast Express, which had been started by the North British Railway from Glasgow Queen Street to Dundee via Crail the previous year. It was withdrawn during the First World War but was reinstated in 1920/21 and existed, with route and time permutations, until the Second World War.

After the second period of hostilities, British Railways reinstated the title on May 23, 1949, giving it to the 7.15am St Andrews-Glasgow Queen Street and 4.07pm return, which ran with the articulated 'Silver Jubilee' coaches for a number of years. The service was summer-only and was most un-express like, calling at every station beyond Leven except Kilconquhar.

For the last three years of its life, it used Glasgow Buchanan Street station and ran for the last time on September 5, 1959.

FLUSHING BOAT TRAIN

NOT to be confused with the 'Flushing Continental' (see next entry), this service was introduced by the South Eastern Railway and ran between London Charing Cross and Folkestone, conveying a single Pullman car in its rake and connecting with steamers for the Dutch port of Flushing (Vlissingen). Prior to 1911, it ran to Queenborough, on the north Kent coast, as that's where the ferries initially sailed from. The train survived the 1923 'Big Four' Grouping but was withdrawn by the Southern Railway.

(THE) FLUSHING CONTINENTAL

ONE of several 'Continental' boat trains run by the LNER to connect with ships at Harwich Parkeston Quay. The others were the 'Antwerp Continental', the 'Day Continental' and the 'Hook Continental.' Their origins dated back to the Great Eastern Railway, which began attaching Pullman cars to its Hook of Holland boat trains circa 1921.

The 'Flushing Continental' differed from its sisters in that it did not originate with the Great Eastern Railway. Before 1927, Zeeland Steam Ship Co ferries to and from the Dutch port of Flushing (Vlissingen) ran to Southern Railway territory at Folkestone, but in January of that year were transferred to Harwich.

At first, un-named trains connected with them, but on September 26, 1927, the LNER introduced the 'Flushing Continental', which included first class and restaurant Pullman cars in a short formation running non-stop to/from London Liverpool Street.

The train, along with all the other 'Continentals', ceased running in September 1939, but after the war, the ferries began sailing from Hook of Holland. As that does not lie in Zeeland, the name of the train was changed in June 1947 to 'The Day Continental'.

'THE FLYING DUTCHMAN'

ALTHOUGH not the first official title, the 'Flying Dutchman' is one of the two oldest train names in the country (the other being 'The Irish Mail'). The train to which it was first applied was the broad gauge Great Western Railway's 9.50am from Paddington to Exeter, which had been introduced in December 1847 and 'flew' between London and Didcot at an average of 57mph. In 1849, its exploits led to it being named after a racehorse that had won the Derby and the St Leger that year, and which itself had been named after a legendary 'ghost ship' and a Wagnerian opera of 1843.

When the schedules were slowed in the 1850s, the name fell out of use until revived on March 1, 1862 for a new and even speedier train, the 11.45am Exeter service, which the GWR claimed as the fastest in the world from 1871 to 1884.

In its early days, the 'Flying Dutchman' (sometimes referred to simply as 'The Dutchman') used the metals of the Bristol & Exeter Railway beyond Bristol, often hauled along that section by the B&E's remarkable Pearson 9ft Singles, which were said "to run very steadily and smoothly at over 70mph". As railway construction expanded westwards, the destination of the express changed to Plymouth and then, briefly, Penzance.

In 1862, the London & South Western Railway introduced a train over its own London-Exeter route that arrived at its destination in 4¾ hours. The GWR therefore changed the departure time of the 'Dutchman' to 11.45 and achieved an arrival in Exeter St David's a ¼ of an hour sooner.

Over the next five years, the competitive nature waned and the timings of the 'Dutchman' became slower, so much so that in November 1867, it was withdrawn altogether, but two years later, the GWR realised it had made an error and reinstated it with its 11.45 departure time, providing it with all-new clerestory stock. Thereafter, the Paddington departure time remained constant for the rest of the train's existence. The train's last run was on May 29, 1892.

Although a photograph did appear in *The Railway Magazine* in 1904 purporting to depict a standard gauge 'Flying Dutchman', it is understood that the train's name ceased to be used after 1892 and it therefore remained a broad gauge train for its entire life.

Picture left: The broad gauge 'Flying Dutchman' at speed. This photo first appeared in *The Railway Magazine* of October 1899.

EUROSTAR LINK

ALTHOUGH 'Eurostar' is a company name and therefore not, strictly speaking, part of this directory, the opening of the Channel Tunnel in 1994 spawned a number of short-lived connecting services to London Waterloo pending the proposed (but ultimately abandoned) 'Regional Eurostar' and 'Night Star' projects.

Two conventional 'Eurostar Link' trains ran using HST stock, one along the East Coast to connect Edinburgh with Waterloo and one along the West Coast route from Manchester Piccadilly. The trains accessed Waterloo via the West London Line but entered the domestic platforms, not the international ones, passengers then transferring to the Eurostar terminus on foot.

The link trains were in action during 1995/6 and, on occasion, were referred to as 'European Connection' services.

(THE) FLYING SCOTSMAN *

The most famous train in

Above: A perfect combination: King's Cross station, 'The Flying Scotsman' and an A4 Pacific named after Sir Nigel Gresley, whose locos did so much to speed up the East Coast. COLOUR-RAIL

Below: The name of the train was painted on the roof for the benefit of airborne newsreel cameramen on May 20, 1932. GETTY IMAGES

THE debate about the most famous train of all would be a long and heated one, but few would argue that 'The Flying Scotsman' would not be the favourite to win.

Not only is it one of the most iconic expresses in the world, it's also one of the oldest, with a history dating back to June 1862, although the title had not been conferred on it at that time and, in fact, didn't appear officially until as late as July 11, 1927.

Until then, the 10am departure from London King's Cross to Edinburgh Waverley and its simultaneous southbound service were known semi-officially as the 'Special Scotch Express'. The terms "Flying Scotsman" (and sometimes "Flying Scotchman") were more in the way of nicknames used by staff and passengers.

The agreement to adopt a formal title came about more easily once the three joint operators of the train along its 393-mile journey – the Great Northern, the North Eastern and the North British railways – had been brought together under the unified management of the LNER in 1923, and the first visible signs came in October 1924 when new rolling stock came into use, bearing carriage roofboards stating 'The Flying Scotsman'. Another three and a half years would pass before headboards began to be carried, however.

An interesting point, not always appreciated even by rail enthusiasts, is that the 1923-built Pacific loco often confused by the public with the train of the same name, was actually christened before the train as it received its nameplates when renumbered 4472 in March 1924.

As for speed, the NB, NE and GN had been straitjacketed by an agreement made in 1895 with the rival West Coast companies (following the outrageously risky 'races to the north') that no railway would cut the London-Glasgow/Edinburgh times below 8¼hrs.

But what the East Coast companies lost in speed over the 37 years to 1932, they gained in quality of rolling stock and by the late-1920s, the LNER's flagship train was equipped not only with all the mods & cons required for serving fine cuisine en route but with a hairdressing salon,

a cocktail bar and a ladies' retiring room. The 1895 agreement had in effect turned long-distance Anglo-Scottish trains from racing yachts into cruise liners and the 'Flying Scotsman' was one of the finest liners there was!

July 11, 1927 was the day the name that had been carried on the roofboards was made official, but the date that proved the most momentous was May 1, 1928. On that day, the LNER turned the summer season 'Flying Scotsman' into the longest non-stop train in the world, using Gresley's innovative corridor tender design to exchange crews en route. Ridiculously, though, the train had to amble along much of the route in order not to break the 8¼-hour agreement between the East and West Coast companies.

The bond was unsustainable and was finally broken in the early 1930s, after which the LNER set about making up for lost time. And how! In November 1934, *Flying Scotsman* the engine became the first steam locomotive in the world officially to break the 100mph record. Speed records were being smashed with regularity at that time and schedules were coming down too; by 1937 'Flying Scotsman' the train had lopped 1¼ hours off its Edinburgh journey time.

An interesting point is that 'Flying Scotsman' headboards could sometimes be seen carried by small engines such as D49 4-4-0s. The reason for that was because the train contained through portions for Aberdeen, Perth and Glasgow, which were detached at Edinburgh and worked forward by locally-based locomotives.

The flurry of renewed competition and higher speeds met with the approval of the travelling public and it was not unknown on some days for the 'Scotsman' to load to 16 bogie vehicles (600 tons) – but even those trains paled into insignificance against those hauled during the war. On some days in the troubled early-1940s, the 'Scotsman' had as many as 22 or 23 coaches for an all-up weight approaching a staggering 800 tons – often handled by a single A4! Despite those burdens, it was one of only a handful of trains to retain its title throughout the war, although the non-stop aspect did cease for the duration,

the world?

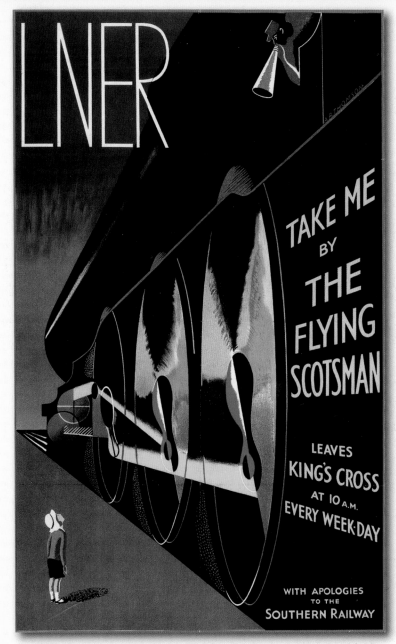

The LNER's advertising executives knew a good idea when they saw it and were not afraid to copy a Southern Railway poster showing a young child talking to an engine driver.

not being resumed until 1948. In that year, the 'Scotsman' set another record when it was diverted for several days because of floods north of Berwick, the route via Kelso creating a 408-mile non-stop journey... a British record.

Gresley and Peppercorn Pacifics maintained the high reputation of the famous 10am express through the 1950s before handing over to Britain's most powerful diesel locomotives, the 'Deltics', in 1962. Those 3,300hp Type 5s – carrying, for a year or so in 1964/65, special golden-coloured 'winged thistles' in lieu of text headboards – enabled the train to be further accelerated and by 1977, the time had been reduced to less than 5½ hours, but those locos in turn yielded to HSTs in May 1978 and timings improved again, to 4hr 35min by the early '80s.

Once locos had disappeared, headboards were no longer deployed, although the name continued in use in every other respect. The big regrettable break with tradition was the decision by BR in 1982 to change the time-honoured 10am start from King's Cross and send 'The Aberdonian' out in that legendary time slot instead.

Salt was rubbed into the purists' wounds as the 'Flying Scotsman' itself then had its journey extended to Aberdeen, calling at Dundee and the relatively small towns of Arbroath, Montrose and Stonehaven. In InterCity Pullman days, a further break with tradition came as the former pride of the East Coast was sent across to the 'auld enemy'

at Glasgow Central, calling at Haymarket and Motherwell.

Upon Privatisation, ECML services were taken over by Great North Eastern Railway, which not only enhanced on-train customer service but applied coats of arms to the sides of its coaches proudly proclaiming 'Route of the Flying Scotsman'.

The next big change came on May 23, 2011, when East Coast, the current operator of the service, re-launched the brand and reliveried locomotive No. 91101 with huge bodyside lettering, even though it was a common-user machine... thus causing many non-cognoscenti to comment that they'd seen the 'Flying Scotsman' in places such as Leeds and Wakefield!

Curiously, East Coast only afforded the title to one train – the 05.40 up service. There is no named balancing turn... the first time in history that this famous train cannot be caught from London.

'THE FLYING WELSHMAN'

IN 1897, *The Railway Magazine* published a feature article on the Great Western Railway's 10am Cardiff to London Paddington service and described it as 'The Flying Welshman' – "one of the finest express trains in the world". As with most titles from the 19th century, it would almost certainly have been an unofficial name.

'FOLKESTONE VESTIBULE LIMITED'

INTRODUCED in 1897, this Pullman train connected London Victoria with the Kentish port and resort of Folkestone. In the same year, the South Eastern Railway introduced the 'Folkestone Car Train' from Charing Cross.

The history of these trains is complex as 'Folkestone Vestibule Limited' was also used as an alternative name for the SER's 'Folkestone Car Train'. Both names were also used as internal company rolling stock designations to distinguish between two types of saloon carriages used on the so-called 'American Car Train' services.

THE FURTHER NORTH EXPRESS

THIS train was introduced by the Highland Railway in the summer of 1906 and ran initially from Inverness to Dornoch, changing later that year to run to Wick.

It was withdrawn during the First World War but restored after the 1923 Grouping and in 1936 was renamed 'The John O' Groat'.

THE FYLDE COAST EXPRESS

See Blackpool & Fylde Coast Express.

THE GALLOWAY ENTERPRISE

LIKE the 'Ayrshire Trader', this was one part of a return service that bore a different title to its balancing working.

Coined by BR's ScotRail sector in 1989/90, the 'Galloway Enterprise' ran from Newcastle to Stranraer Harbour via Carlisle, while its return working from Stranraer was known as 'The Tyne Enterprise'. The trains were usually formed of Class 156s and both titles were dropped in winter 1997/98.

GARDEN CITIES & CAMBRIDGE BUFFET EXPRESS

(See Cambridge Buffet Express).

(GATWICK EXPRESS)

(*Brand name*): A generic term coined by British Rail in 1984 for its high-frequency London Victoria-Gatwick Airport dedicated shuttle service. Upon Privatisation in 1996, the name became that of a train operating company.

'THE GERALD OF WALES' (Y GERALLT GYMRO)

SOMETIMES abbreviated to 'The Gerald', this was a name Arriva Trains Wales's through Cardiff-Holyhead service was known by when it was launched with Welsh Assembly Government backing in 2008. The loco-hauled service recalled a 12th century Archdeacon of Brecon (a legendary Welsh traveller), but the name did not appear in the national timetables.

THE GLASGOW EXECUTIVE

A SHORT-lived Glasgow Central-London Euston service which operated for one timetable term only, 1984, leaving Euston at 16.50 and Glasgow at 17.10.

Continental elegance on rails

SELECTING a single titled train to represent each of the 'Big Four' would be an invidious task, but assuming that 'The Flying Scotsman' would win the LNER section, the general consensus for the others would probably result in 'The Royal Scot', 'The Cornish Riviera' and, for the Southern... the 'Golden Arrow'.

The 'Arrow' was the ultimate boat train – oozing opulence, romance and the promise of far-off climes. It was also unique in that it had a doppelgänger on the other side of the Channel at Calais – a train bearing the French equivalent of the title ('Flèche d'Or'), which took passengers on to Paris.

However, unlike the 'Night Ferry', the carriages of the 'Arrow' did not travel across the Channel.

Like many other named expresses in Britain, it was based on a service that had been in operation since the pre-Grouping era but which only gained its title some years later, in this case 1929.

On May 15 of that year, the Southern Railway began running an all-first class Pullman train from London Victoria to Dover Marine to match the 'Flèche d'Or', which had been running from Paris to Calais since 1926. Although some history books claim the name was taken from that of an American speed record-holding car, 'Golden Arrow' was in fact a translation of the French train title and in early advertising it  was always shown as 'Golden Arrow Limited'. It left London at 11am and returned in the afternoon.

At Dover quayside, passengers transferred to a first class steamer and, after a 75-minute crossing, boarded the Nord (later SNCF) version of the train.

In the four years immediately prior to the wartime shutdown, however, the port on the French side was changed to Boulogne, meaning that the London-bound train on the British side had to collect its passengers from Folkestone – and that meant climbing the ferocious 1-in-30 incline out of Folkestone Harbour station, a job usually entrusted to a trio of sturdy tank locos.

The situation was reversed between 1952 and 1960 with Folkestone becoming the outward port and Dover the inward one.

The post-war years saw the train restored to all-Pullman status (it had been reduced to four such cars

between 1932 and 1939 because of the trade slump) and Bulleid and Standard Pacifics take over.

Stewarts Lane depot made a point of keeping regular locos for the 'Arrow' and turning them out in beautifully polished condition, not only to match a partly new ten-car Pullman set provided to mark the Festival of Britain in 1951, but to reflect the romance of foreign travel and be in keeping with the huge gilt arrows affixed to the front and sides of the engine for this most special of duties.

The end of steam on the 'Arrow' came on June 11, 1961 and with it went the large embellishments. The rather modest-looking Bo-Bo electric locos that took over carried smaller adornments and fibreglass headboards, but in BR's increasingly corporate 'blue' era, a set of deluxe coaches retained specifically for one return trip became something of an anachronism and the 'Golden Arrow' was finally laid to rest on September 30, 1972.

Top of page: With the huge arrow on the loco's air-smoothed bodyside, the circular headboard on the smokebox and the flags of Britain and France above the bufferbeam, the 'Golden Arrow' makes a magnificent sight as it leaves Dover Marine behind 'Battle of Britain' Pacific No. 34085 *501 Squadron* in June 1959. COLOUR-RAIL

Above: Whenever 'Britannia' or rebuilt Bulleid Pacifics were deployed, a smaller arrow was fitted to the smoke deflectors. No. 70004 *William Shakespeare* in full cry at Folkestone Warren in 1953. RAIL PHOTOPRINTS

Left: The takeover of the train by Class 71 electric locos resulted in a much smaller and less ostentatious headboard, as seen on August 19, 1962. R A LISSENDEN

Above: 'The Granite City', a sobriquet for Aberdeen, provided an ideal title for a service between there and Glasgow. At 5.30pm on July 29, 1953, 'Black Five' No. 44930 gets ready to leave for Glasgow Buchanan Street.
BRIAN MORRISON

(THE) GOLDEN HIND *

A DIESEL-hauled Plymouth-Paddington express introduced by BR's Western Region on June 15, 1964.

Hauled by a 2,700hp 'Western' class locomotive paired with a seven-coach rake, it left Plymouth North Road at 7.05am and reached London in a then record time of 3hrs 50mins. In 1972, the service was extended to Penzance and later became an HST duty, slashing the Plymouth time to 3hrs 15min.

Perhaps appropriately, the 'Hind' (in loco-hauled days) was one of the few trains to bear its title on the rear carriage vestibule covers and it was still being displayed in the late-1960s, having by then been supplemented by BR corporate Inter-City branding. (Perhaps inappropriately, however, the train has for almost half a century been a regular butt of humour among railwaymen, who habitually refer to it as 'The Brass Arse'.)

The train's title is, in fact, taken from the name of Sir Francis Drake's sailing ship of the 1570s.

In 1983, the service was re-launched as the 'Golden Hind Executive' and four years later, re-named again, this time as the 'Golden Hind Pullman' but in 1993 it reverted to its original title (with the addition of the definite article) and still runs today, as First Great Western's 18.03 Paddington-Plymouth-Penzance and 05.05 return.

GOLDEN SANDS EXPRESS

THIS was not a holiday train as such (see p57), but a shuttle service operated by the LMS three times a day between Rhyl and Llandudno in the summer of 1931.

The train, which carried a headboard and often loaded to six coaches hauled by an ex-LNWR 4-4-0, mainly conveyed holidaymakers along the North Wales Coast, calling at Colwyn Bay and other intermediate resorts, but it is not certain how many seasons it ran for.

The name was briefly resurrected as a local initiative in BR London Midland Region days.

THE GRAMPIAN

NAMED after the range of mountains dominating the part of Scotland north of the central lowlands, this was one of the oldest official train titles in the country, being first coined in 1905 by the Caledonian Railway to describe a prestigious Glasgow Buchanan Street-Aberdeen restaurant car express formed of new 12-wheeled corridor stock. In those days, its full title was the 'Grampian Corridor Express'.

The Glasgow-Edinburgh-Dundee-Aberdeen route was the busiest long-distance main line within Scotland and the CR was in competition with the North British Railway for its trade, hence the need for high-quality rolling stock and glamorous train titles.

The name was discontinued upon the outbreak of the First World War, but was revived as 'The Grampian' in 1937 and then again in June 1962 by BR's Scottish Region to describe its 8.25am Glasgow-Aberdeen and 1.30pm return, one of a quartet of 'three-hour' expresses hauled between the two cities by Gresley A4s and other Pacifics from then until September 1966, when the services were dieselised.

THE GRANITE CITY

TAKING its title from the colloquial name for Aberdeen, 'The Granite City Express' was introduced in 1906 by the Caledonian Railway to describe a pair of restaurant car expresses on the Edinburgh Princes Street-Aberdeen line.

That name ceased in 1914, but the Caledonian's successor, the LMS, resurrected it and shortened it to 'The Granite City' and it made its first run as such on July 17, 1933, running from Glasgow to Aberdeen.

When the Second World War broke out six years later, the title was removed but was resurrected on May 23, 1949.

In the early to mid-1960s, A4 Pacifics, drafted in for the purpose or cascaded from English main line duties, took over some of the Glasgow-Aberdeen duties and reeled the southbound run off in three hours (departing Aberdeen at 5.15pm and arriving at 8.15), but those services were dieselised from September 1966 and the following year brought closure of the ex-Caledonian main line through Coupar Angus and Forfar, meaning that the 'Granite City' had to be re-routed via the coast road through Dundee and Arbroath.

As an effect of this, the train officially lost its title on May 4, 1968, although the name is understood to have continued in partial use until 1977.

In 1991, the title was formally reinstated to specify a Glasgow-Aberdeen DMU service, only to be withdrawn again in 1995.

GRANVILLE SPECIAL EXPRESS

THE first train in Britain to carry an *official* name, the 'Granville Special Express' was launched by the South Eastern Railway on December 22, 1876 and took its name from the Granville Hotel at St Lawrence-on-Sea, near Ramsgate.

The service, which didn't appear in Bradshaw's timetable until March of the following year, initially left London Charing Cross every Friday at 3.45pm and

Right: A little artistic licence is evident from this 1879 drawing. The carriage roofboards show it to be the South Eastern Railway's 'Granville Special Private Express' and the station is the SER's London Charing Cross, but close inspection of the engine's cabside will reveal the letters LCDR. The latter railway had begun competing with the SER for the Granville Hotel trade the previous year and it is believed that the drawing was 'doctored' by the hotel for publication in its own house journal.

returned from Ramsgate each Monday morning at
8.40am, although it was subsequently to undergo
numerous timing, route and name amendments.

(On April 1, 1878, the fiercely-competitive London,
Chatham & Dover Railway introduced its own, similarly-
named train – see next entry).

In October 1878, the SER's down train became the
'Granville Express', although the up service retained the
full title containing the word 'Special'. Both trains ceased
at the end of May 1880, but the 'Granville Express' title
was reintroduced by the South Eastern for a daily (Mon-
Sat) service in both directions on April 1, 1884.

Over the next few seasons, the title was used on and
off (and with various suffixes, such as Deal, Walmer,
Shorncliffe, Folkestone and Sandgate) until June 1904
when it was finally discontinued. By then, the SER had
merged with the rival LCDR (in 1899) and the expresses
during those last few years were jointly operated. (From
1888 to 1904 some of the 'Granville Express's timings had
been taken by a new train, the 'Kent Coast Express'.)

GRANVILLE AND WESTGATE-ON-SEA SPECIAL EXPRESS

THIS was a completely separate train from the 'Granville
Express' and was operated by a different company, the
London, Chatham & Dover Railway (LCDR). It ran from
London Victoria to Ramsgate via Faversham and remained in
operation until the merger of the LCDR and the SER in 1899,
after which the service was run jointly by the resultant South
Eastern & Chatham Railway.

The title was resurrected by the SECR in July 1921
and the Southern Railway continued it until July 1927.

GREENORE BOAT EXPRESS

A SERVICE that ran from London Euston to Holyhead
harbour in LNWR days and was named after the Irish port
with whose ferries it made connection. It was withdrawn at
the outbreak of the First World War in 1914 and never
reinstated.

(THE) HARROGATE PULLMAN

THE story behind this train's inception is an unusual one.

Prior to the Grouping, the Great Eastern Railway had
successfully operated a fleet of Pullman cars on its
'Continental' boat trains (see separate entries), but had
encountered difficulty making them pay on the other routes
it operated in the mainly agricultural area of East Anglia.

So when the GER came under the control of the LNER
in 1923, the latter set about finding a more sensible use
for the luxury vehicles. The Yorkshire spa town of
Harrogate had long been a well-heeled community and so
the LNER agreed with the cars' owners, the Pullman Car
Co, that six surplus vehicles would be transferred to the
GN section and formed into a King's Cross-Leeds-
Harrogate-Newcastle express – the LNER's first
all-Pullman train.

The new train was inaugurated on July 9, 1923,
running Mondays to Saturdays. In July 1925, it was made
non-stop to Harrogate over the 199 miles from London
and its northern terminus was extended to Edinburgh. It
was renamed the 'Harrogate and Edinburgh Pullman'
(known unofficially but more popularly as the 'Edinburgh
Pullman').

On December 1, 1927, it was officially renamed the
'Queen of Scots'.

(THE) HARROGATE SUNDAY PULLMAN

THIS train was introduced on May 9, 1928, replacing the
'Weekend Pullman' and running on Sundays between King's
Cross, Leeds Central and Harrogate. It used 'Queen of Scots'
stock, which would otherwise have been lying idle in London
for the day.

To start with, there was a through portion from
Bradford, attached at Leeds, on the southbound working
only, but from July 13, 1929, the northbound service
gained a Bradford portion too.

The train was suspended on September 10, 1939 for

Above: A1 No. 60148
Aboyeur heads south with
'The Harrogate Sunday
Pullman' at Beeston
Junction, near Leeds,
on April 15, 1961.
GAVIN MORRISON

HARROGATE AND
EDINBURGH
PULLMAN

See Edinburgh
Pullman

Sadly, titled train headboards are no longer used on regular service trains in Britain, but they do continue to be seen on the main line thanks to their use by privately-organised railtours and charter trains. Some of the names are newly-devised appelations coined for that particular one-off railtour (e.g. 'The Lincolnshire Poacher', 'The Dreaming Spires Express' or 'The Retford Rover'), but many other modern railtour operators happily re-use traditional names on traditional curved headboards. An excellent line-up of such titles is pictured on display at Barrow Hill roundhouse. Left to right: The 'Yorkshire Pullman' on A1 No. 60163 *Tornado*; 'The North Eastern' on A2 No. 60532 *Blue Peter*; 'The Elizabethan' on A4 No. 60007 *Sir Nigel Gresley* and 'The Heart of Midlothian' on A4 No. 60009 *Sir Nigel Gresley*.
ROBIN STEWART-SMITH

the war, but reinstated on June 11, 1950. It continued into the diesel era, not being withdrawn until March 5, 1967.

It is interesting to note that in the early years, the Pullman Car Company referred to it in its own publicity as "the Sunday working of the 'West Riding Pullman'."

THE HARROVIAN
THIS was a real rarity – an officially-named train running regularly on what is now the London Underground system.

In service between 1911 and 1932, it was a Metropolitan/District Railway train departing from South Harrow at 8.15am (later 8.20) and running to Mansion House.

THE HEART LINE
ALTHOUGH it sounds like a brand name, this was the title of a long-distance HST service that ran from Edinburgh to Plymouth/Penzance for one year only, 1982.

'THE HARWICH BOAT TRAIN'
(*Descriptive term*): An informal term for the various services that ran between Harwich Parkeston Quay and the North-West, whose official titles changed so frequently that passengers and rail staff had trouble keeping up with them!

THE HEART OF MIDLOTHIAN
EDINBURGH lies in the heart of the old county of Midlothian and this title – which is also the name of one of the city's football clubs – was one of those chosen by BR to mark the Festival of Britain in 1951.

The train selected for a release from anonymity was the 2pm King's Cross-Edinburgh Waverley and its southbound balancing turn (whose departure time was also 2pm). Brand new Mk1 stock in BR carmine & cream livery was provided and Pacific power supplied, putting the train into the upper echelon of East Coast expresses.

It was launched on June 18, 1951. Six years later, from September 16, 1957, the service was experimentally extended to Perth via Falkirk and Stirling. In that same year, BR had also given Perth another named train – 'The Fair Maid'– but the people of that city seemed not to appreciate a direct link with London and both expresses

were withdrawn after just a year, due to poor patronage.

The 'Heart of Midlothian' reverted to Edinburgh and in the summer of 1962 became part of the 'Deltic' revolution, enjoying substantial accelerations despite its 12 or 14-coach loadings until disappearing from the scene on May 6, 1968, in a general BR purge on individuality.

(HEATHROW EXPRESS AND HEATHROW CONNECT)
(*Brand names*): High-frequency shuttle services between London Paddington and Heathrow Airport.

THE HEBRIDEAN
KYLE of Lochalsh is one of the furthest extremities of the British network, lying 263 miles by rail even from Glasgow, but it was graced with not one, but two named trains.

'The Hebridean', launched in 1933, was an LMS breakfast car train that left Inverness at 7.25am, after waiting for a through sleeping car from Glasgow to be attached, and arrived in the Kyle at 10.31. In the passing loop at Achnasheen, it would have passed its sister train, 'The Lewisman'.

'The Hebridean' had a quick turn-round at Kyle and was ready to leave again at 10.45, getting back to Inverness at 2 o' clock.

In winter months, only two of those four workings operated, which meant the restaurant car being shunted over from one train to the other each time they reached Achnasheen.

After the war, 'The Lewisman' was withdrawn, but British Railways decided to continue with 'The Hebridean' and even to provide the westbound train with an observation car so that passengers could enjoy the splendid Highland scenery and watch as the eastbound 'Hebridean' passed them in Achnasheen loop.

Departure time from Inverness was changed to 10.40am and the train became a fixture in the Scottish Region calendar right into the diesel era when BRCW Type 2 diesels, and then English Electric Type 3s, began to work the trains that had been the province of Stanier 'Black Fives' since 1953.

The title was revived between 1982 and 1987 for a

mid-morning Inverness-Kyle observation car service and late afternoon return, which was known by a slightly different title from 1988 to September 1993 (see next entry).

HEBRIDEAN HERITAGE
THIS was the amended name of 'The Hebridean' (see previous entry) from 1988 until 1991/92 when it was further renamed, to 'Highland Heritage'. For a while, the train contained an observation saloon converted from a DMU vehicle.

(HELENSBURGH EXPRESS)
(*Brand name*): Introduced by Strathclyde Transport in 1984 to describe the limited-stop services on the electrified Glasgow High Street-Helensburgh route. Discontinued in 1986.

THE HIBERNIAN
IN summer 1987, British Rail adopted this title for the 01.50 Fishguard Harbour-Paddington HST and 09.30 return. The same name was also applied to the 14.10 up and 22.40 down services. The title disappeared temporarily in winter 1987/88 and reappeared between summer 1988 and summer 1990, after which it became a Sundays-only service. It was dropped permanently in September '91.

THE HIGHLAND CHIEFTAIN *
'THE Highland Chieftain' is one of four named passenger trains currently operated by East Coast and is by far and away the fastest through working ever between London King's Cross and Inverness.

Operated by HSTs, it leaves London at midday and arrives in the Highland capital, 581 miles away, just over eight hours later, at 20.11 (20.19 on Sundays).

The times of the southbound Mon-Sat service are 07.55 from Inverness, arriving in London at 15.54 (15.57 on Saturdays). Departure on Sunday mornings is delayed until 09.40, giving a 17.57 arrival at King's Cross.

The northbound service leaves King's Cross at 12.00 seven days a week, with arrival in Inverness at 20.11 (20.19 on Sundays).

The train's title dates to 1984 when it began life as British Rail's 07.20 Inverness-King's Cross and 12.00 northbound. At one point in its existence, it ran from Inverness only as far as Newcastle, reaching that city via Carlisle.

HIGHLAND ENTERPRISE
A BRITISH Rail diesel loco-hauled service between Edinburgh and Inverness that lasted from 1991 until 1994.

HIGHLAND EXPRESS
THERE were two 'Highland Expresses', one operated by the Midland Railway and active on the St Pancras-Inverness route in pre-Grouping days, and the other introduced by the London & North Western Railway between Euston and Inverness circa 1880s.

HIGHLAND HERITAGE
A TITLE carried by the 10.15 Inverness to Kyle of Lochalsh and its afternoon return, which was in effect from May to September 1992.

(THE) HIGHLANDMAN
BY the late-1920s, the 'Aberdonian' had become such a heavy train that, in summer, it was split into two sections, one of which departed King's Cross 15 minutes earlier at 7.25pm and included carriages for Fort William, Inverness and Nairn.

Interestingly, this relief train was given a name of its own… and a completely different one at that – the 'Highlandman'.

The maiden run of the newly-entitled train took place on July 11, 1927 and from 1932 onwards, it began to carry a headboard, but for how long is unknown. It ceased to run a week after the start of the Second World War.

Above: A named train that didn't survive into the British Railways era was the 'Highlandman', which, somewhat unusually, was granted an identity of its own even though it started life as a mere relief to the 'Aberdonian'. It lasted from 1927 to 1939 and is seen waiting to leave King's Cross behind a Gresley non-streamlined Pacific.
J HUBBACK

TITLED TRAINS HAULED BY TANK ENGINES

Prairie tank No. 5517 on the 'Cambrian Coast Express', July 1958

NAMED trains were hauled by tank engines more frequently than might be expected.

Among those occasionally or regularly worked by tanks were the 'Cambridge Buffet Express'; the St Ives portion of 'The Cornish Riviera'; the Pwllheli portion of the 'Cambrian Coast Express'; the Cheltenham-Gloucester section of the 'Cheltenham Spa Express'; the Torrington, Bude, Seaton, Sidmouth and Exmouth portions of the 'Atlantic Coast Express'; the Pwllheli/Portmadoc portions of 'The Welshman'; the Walton-on-the-Naze portion of the 'Clacton Interval Service'; the Leamington-Stratford portion of 'The William Shakespeare' and the Bradford portions of 'The West Riding' and the 'Yorkshire Pullman'.

(THE) HOOK CONTINENTAL

THIS was one of several 'Continentals' run by the LNER to connect with ships at Harwich Parkeston Quay. Others included the 'Antwerp Continental', the 'Day Continental' and the 'Flushing Continental'.

Their origins dated back to the Great Eastern Railway, which began attaching Pullman cars to its Hook of Holland boat trains from 1921.

Over the years, the train went by several title variants, including 'Hook of Holland Express' (down direction only) between 1919 and 1926, and plain 'Hook of Holland'. The 'Hook Continental' title was carried between 1927 and 1939, apart from a gap between July 1932 and July 1937 when it was merged with the Antwerp service and known as the 'Hook & Antwerp Continental'.

The cessation of public sailings to Europe during the war meant that it did not run for six years after September 1939, but it was reinstated (without the Antwerp appendage) on November 14, 1945 – making it the first titled train in Britain to be revived after the hostilities. At first, it ran thrice weekly, then daily from 1946, continuing right up until May 10, 1987, by which time the ex-GE main line had been electrified.

On at least one occasion, this provided the very rare sight of a steam engine-style headboard being carried by a Class 86 AC electric locomotive (see picture on right).

In the 1986 timetable, the train of this name was the 07.40 Parkeston Quay to Liverpool Street and 19.50 return

Right: The rare sight of a curved steam-age headboard on an AC electric locomotive, pictured passing Colchester on May 12, 1986.
Photograph by MALCOLM ROOT

Above: Headboards were often attached on shed to ensure they weren't inadvertently left behind! B1 No. 1149 is seen being prepared at Parkeston MPD before taking 'The Hook Continental' to London in LNER days.
Painting by MALCOLM ROOT

THE HIGHLANDS CAR SLEEPER

A SLEEPING car service that ran via the East Coast route to Inverness and which was in service until at least the early 1970s. It ran three times a week and was almost invariably hauled by a Class 40 diesel-electric in the 1960s.

THE HIGHWAYMAN

MOST trains in this survey run to a London terminus or at least to a coastal resort or major junction. 'The Highwayman' was different, for the London end of its journey was Finsbury Park station, 2½ miles outside King's Cross.

Launched by British Rail on May 4, 1970, the train originated in Newcastle at 9.15am, arrived at Finsbury Park at 3.12pm and offered heavily-discounted fares at a flat rate of just 175 pence, but only if booked in advance. The northbound working departed from Finsbury Park at 9.25am and the train, usually hauled by a Class 40, also incorporated an ex-LNER buffet car.

It is believed that BR's marketing whizzkids chose the name 'Highwayman' to draw attention to the fact that the fares could be considered as 'daylight robbery'! That may well have been the case, for the prices proved unsustainable and the service was axed in October 1971 after just two summer seasons.

(HOLIDAYMAKER EXPRESS)

(*Brand name*): Although a quick glance at a 1980s summer timetable might suggest that this was a titled train, further inspection will reveal that there were numerous trains running on diverse routes under this British Rail marketing title – from Scottish, Northern and Midlands industrial cities to resorts such as Paignton, Poole, Portsmouth Harbour, Tenby and Weymouth.

Some ran overnight, the 22.05 from York not arriving in Portsmouth until 06.18 the following morning, for example. By the 1990s, the title had changed to 'InterCity Holidaymaker'.

HOOK & ANTWERP CONTINENTAL

A TRAIN that combined the 'Hook Continental' and the 'Antwerp Continental' between 1932 and 1937, during the great pre-war economic depression of the 1930s. See separate entries for both trains.

HOOK OF HOLLAND EXPRESS

See 'Hook Continental'.

THE HULL EXECUTIVE *

THE huge city of Kingston-upon-Hull has traditionally been something of a railway backwater where passenger services are concerned. Even in the 21st century, it took an open access operator, Hull Trains, to provide it with a decent and frequent direct link with London.

In terms of prestige services, there had been only 'The Hull Pullman' in 1967 (see next entry) and, 11 years later, 'The Hull Executive'. This was the fourth of five 'Executive' trains operated by BR's Eastern Region. Comprising just eight Mk2 coaches and hauled by a 3,300hp 'Deltic', it was launched in May 1978 as a replacement for the 'Hull Pullman' and was aimed at businessmen from the then-new county of Humberside.

Executives could be in London in less than three hours and the train thus became well patronised, especially as passengers could purchase such miscellaneous items as car parking and meals at the same time as the ticket. The 17.05 return from King's Cross was for a while the fastest timetabled loco-hauled train in the country with an average speed of 91.3mph.

The 'Hull Executive' was 'Deltic'-hauled until yielding to the HST revolution in January 1981 and, for a four-year period between 1991 and 1994, ran under the name of 'The Hull Pullman'. It then reverted to its own epithet and still runs today as an East Coast HST service, up to the capital at 07.00 and returning to Hull at 17.19.

THE HULL PULLMAN

UNTIL 1967, this city of some 300,000 inhabitants had to make do with a four-coach portion of 'The Yorkshire Pullman', but that year British Rail decided to give Kingston-upon-Hull a Pullman service of its own.

'The Hull Pullman' began running in March that year and continued until May 1978 when it was replaced by the 'Hull Executive' (see above), although for four years between 1991 and 1994, the equivalent of the 'Hull Executive' ran under the 'Hull Pullman' name.

HUMBER-LINCS EXECUTIVE

THIS was an HST working introduced in 1984 and designed to put the city of Lincoln on the business commuter map with an early morning service.

Sometimes known simply as the 'Humber-Lincs', it actually started from Cleethorpes and the return leg left King's Cross at 5.13pm. The train was discontinued in 1993.

A similar early morning Lincoln service has been revived by the East Coast TOC in 2011, again with an HST, although this time it carries no name.

ILFRACOMBE BOAT EXPRESS

NOT, as the title might suggest, a Devonian service, this train was operated in Wales by the Barry Railway and ran from Cardiff Riverside to Barry Pier. It was operational from 1905 to 1909.

Running on a regular basis in summers only along the 8¾-mile line, it left Cardiff at 9.35am to connect with a 10.10am sailing to Ilfracombe, north Devon.

The 'Humber-Lincs Executive' (off its usual route at York!)

Waiting in platform 7 at King's Cross on January 3, 1981, is 'Deltic' No. 55007 *Pinza* with 'The Hull Executive', which was inaugurated in 1978 as a replacement for the 'Hull Pullman'. RAIL PHOTOPRINTS

THE INTER-CITY

Train that lent its name to a brand

IT is perhaps not fully appreciated by younger readers that what is widely thought of as a modern era marketing brand actually started life as a steam-hauled train name as long ago as 1950.

'The Inter-City' was introduced on September 25 that year as a response by the Western Region of BR to the popularity of the 9.10am London-Birmingham express. It was decided not only to run a relief as far as Wolverhampton, departing at 9am with a return at 4.25pm, but to grant that train its own title. The fact that the service was to call at Birmingham too justified the title (Wolverhampton had not at that time been afforded official city status), although the headboard carried the coats of arms of all three communities. In 1962, the service was extended to the city of Chester.

The end for 'The Inter-City' in its original guise came on June 11, 1965, in order to make way for British Rail's use of the title as its new marketing brand – one that has remained in use to the present day.

When this photo was taken in Wolverhampton on July 20, 1954, no-one could have had any idea that the title would become such a widespread brand name later in the century. The loco is 'King' 4-6-0 No. 6000 *King George V*. (On the right is a Western Region handbill publicising the train's timings.) BRIAN MORRISON

THIS extremely rare shot of an HST power car carrying a steam-age metal headboard was taken at Holyhead on May 21, 2004, during the last week of Virgin HST running to the North Wales port.
CHRIS MILNER

(INTER-CITY EXECUTIVE)

(*Brand name*): A generic term introduced by BR InterCity in the 1980s. Also used to describe the sector's new corporate livery.

(INTER-CITY HOLIDAYMAKER)

(*Brand name*): A generic term for numerous BR expresses (many on cross-country routes) in the early 1990s. Formerly 'Holidaymaker Express'.

'THE INTER-VARSITY'

IN the days when the two great university cities of Oxford and Cambridge were linked by a direct railway line, this through train ran over the London & North Western Railway-built route. Its name is thought to have been unofficial.

THE IRISH MAIL (VIA HOLYHEAD)

OF all the titled passenger trains in Britain, this is believed to be the oldest as it dates back to 1848 – yet officially it's only 85 years old because (like another long-established train, 'The Flying Scotsman'), it wasn't formally christened until 1927.

The history of 'The Irish Mail' is complicated too; from 1906, there were two completely different trains with the same name, one running on LNWR metals via the North Wales line to Holyhead and the other on the GWR via the South Wales route to Fishguard (see next entry).

There were also two different trains on the Holyhead route itself – one in the morning, leaving Euston circa 8.45am and an evening sleeping car service departing 12 hours later, with corresponding up trains for both.

Once travelling post offices had been introduced into the services, the mailbag pick-up and drop-off apparatus began to be used at numerous locations along the route.

The strategic importance of the route meant that the 'Irish Mail' was kept in operation throughout the war, although its frequency was halved and records differ as to whether it retained its title or not.

It was non-stop, but by the time the war ended, competition from aircraft was such that the evening train was reinstated only during the summer months.

The next major upheaval was brought about by the West Coast electrification scheme in the early-1960s, which saw a stop forced upon the 'non-stop' in Basford Hall marshalling yard to change engines from electric to diesel.

The last titled run in its original guise took place on May 12, 1985, but the title was later revived by InterCity West Coast, both with and without the definite article. The named service continued into the Virgin Trains era, but was dropped at the end of the 20th century.

THE IRISH MAIL (VIA FISHGUARD)

AS mentioned in the preceding entry, there were two completely different forms of the 'Irish Mail'. This was the Great Western Railway version, which ran from Paddington to Fishguard, in south Wales.

It was launched in 1906 and, as on the rival North Wales Coast route, there were two boat trains a day, one from London in the morning (times differed over the years) and another roughly 12 hours later, with corresponding up trains… the latter often requiring bankers to get the heavy trains up the 1-in-50 ruling grades out of Fishguard.

Progress has since rendered the carrying of mail via boat train obsolete and the train last ran in 1939.

THE IRISHMAN

ONE of a surprisingly high number of named trains ending in 'man', this one was an LMS service that ran from Glasgow St Enoch to Stranraer to connect with steamers sailing for Larne, in Northern Ireland.

A year-round restaurant car train, it was launched on July 17, 1933 and ran over the steeply-graded ex-Glasgow & South Western Railway route.

The train, which was nicknamed "The Glesca Paddy" by those familiar with it, ceased running on September 10, 1939, but was reintroduced on May 23, 1949 and continued until March 5, 1967 – by which time it had become something of an oddity… a titled DMU.

The diesel units had taken over many of the passenger services on the line from 1958 and 'The Irishman' was no exception, but it's not known whether the headboard was ever carried by such a unit.

THE IRISH MANCUNIAN

A SERVICE (at first loco-hauled, then DMU-formed) that began running between Holyhead and Manchester/Stockport in 1993. It disappeared from the timetable in 1998.

IRISH NIGHT EXPRESS

A Euston-Holyhead service in LNWR days. There was also a matching 'Day Express'.

ISLE OF MAN BOAT EXPRESS

THERE were two trains of this name, both connecting with ferries to the Isle of Man but from opposite directions; one ran between London Paddington and Birkenhead harbour while the other operated between Glasgow and Ardrossan harbour.

THE JACOBITE

ALTHOUGH this name is today widely associated with the steam-hauled summer service along the Fort William-Mallaig line, it is a less well-known fact that from 1984-86 it was also the title of a British Rail Fridays-only service between

Inverness and Edinburgh, formed of a shortened Edinburgh-Glasgow Mk2 push-pull set and powered by a Class 47/7, calling at Aviemore, Pitlochry, Perth, Stirling, Falkirk Grahamston and Haymarket.

With regard to today's steam-hauled service, preservation era trains are not included in this survey, but an exception has been made for 'The Jacobite' because it and its predecessors, 'The Lochaber' and 'The West Highlander', have been running to a regular timetable on a main line route for more than a quarter of a century. The summer-only service began on the West Highland line in 1984 and this year's timings see it leave Fort William at 10.15 with an extra high-summer only service at 14.30.

THE JOHN O' GAUNT

NAMED after the 14th century Duke of Lancaster, this West Coast electric loco-hauled train was introduced by InterCity and plied between Lancaster and London Euston between 1988 and 1990.

THE JOHN O' GROAT

AS its title suggests, this (along with 'The Orcadian') was the most northerly titled train on the British standard gauge network. It was formerly known as the 'Further North Express' and was introduced by the LMS on May 4, 1936. Containing a restaurant car, it left Wick for Inverness at 10.10am and returned at 4.10pm. It did not survive beyond the Second World War.

THE JOHN PEEL

A 1980s British Rail service between Euston and Carlisle that was named not after the Liverpudlian radio disc jockey but after a Cumberland-born huntsman who died in 1854 and is buried in the churchyard of St Kentigern's church, Caldbeck.

It ran as an up train only from May 16, 1988, leaving Carlisle at 06.00 but the name had disappeared within a year.

'THE JOLLY FISHERMAN'

AN unofficial name for a series of summer-only timetabled loco-hauled trains run by BR to Skegness from Leicester, Nottingham and Derby in the 1980s/early 1990s. The service was often referred to by its passengers as the "Skeggie Flyer".

Below: To mark the 25th anniversary of Her Majesty's reign, BR's Eastern Region turned Class 47 No. 47164 out with a huge bodyside Union flag and used it to haul a specially named train, 'The Jubilee', which plied between London Liverpool Street and Norwich in the summer of 1977. (See next page)
G R MORTIMER

Above: 'The Kentish Belle'
is hurried through Bickley
by N15 class 4-6-0 No.
30767 on August 5, 1957.
R C RILEY

THE JUBILEE

TO celebrate the Queen's silver jubilee in 1977, BR Eastern Region decided to name the 08.30 Liverpool Street-Norwich and 15.48 return. A suitably ornate headboard was devised and the inaugural run took place on June 8 with the intention of running for just a week, but the public reaction to the service was so favourable that it continued until July 2.

To haul the trains, Stratford depot turned out two Class 47s, Nos. 47163/164, emblazoned with huge union flags on their body sides.

'THE JUNIOR SCOTSMAN'

AN unofficial name for the 10.05am King's Cross-Edinburgh, so called because it traditionally left London five minutes after the main 'Flying Scotsman' and acted as a relief to its 'parent' train. The name originated in LNER days.

Occasionally, the train continued from Edinburgh to Glasgow and often included an Aberdeen portion. In the mid-1950s, its London departure time changed to 10.10 and then 11.00.

KENT COAST EXPRESS

FROM October 1, 1888, the South Eastern Railway renamed its 8am Margate to Charing Cross service the 'Kent Coast Express'. Until then it had been the 'Granville Express' (or more specifically the 'Granville, Deal & Walmer Express'). In common with the fickle nature of train namings in those late Victorian days, the title was dropped for the following summer but reintroduced in October 1889, then withdrawn again for the down service in summer 1894 but resumed again in the October.

It continued until July 1, 1904, when it was dropped for good, although the service continued to operate. (Variations on the name over the years included 'Kent Coast and Canterbury Express' , 'Dover, Deal and Kent Coast Express' and 'Herne Bay and Kent Coast Express'.)

To prevent confusion among future historians, it should be pointed out that until its merger with the SER in 1899, the London, Chatham & Dover Railway also used the term 'Kent Coast Express' for some of its own services, resulting in the histories of this, the 'Granville Express' and the 'Cliftonville Express' being intertwined and thus extremely complicated.

(THE) KENTISH BELLE

THE origins of this Pullman train lay in two earlier Kent Pullman services (the 'Thanet Pullman Limited' and the 'Thanet Belle'). After the 1950 season of the latter service, the Southern Region decided to widen its sphere of operation by adding through coaches for Canterbury East, but as that city did not lie in the Isle of Thanet, the name was changed to reflect the train's wider orbit.

The first day of operation for the 'Kentish Belle' was July 2, 1951. Departure time from London Victoria was 11.30am (3.05pm on Saturdays) and the up service left Ramsgate at 5.05pm (6.15 on Saturdays).

The Canterbury section, which required a stop at Faversham to detach them, was discontinued after just one season, but the Southern Region did not revert to the old name and the service continued until September 14, 1958, when it fell victim to the Kent Coast electrification scheme.

LAKE DISTRICT EXPRESS

A MIDLAND Railway service from London St Pancras to Penrith (and onward to Edinburgh), inaugurated in 1910.

THE LAKES EXPRESS

TODAY, the West Coast Main Line has only one branch into

Below: A panoramic view
of Watford Junction station
in 1950s as 'Princess Royal'
Pacific No. 46207 Princess
Arthur of Connaught races
through with 'The Lakes
Express'. COLOUR-RAIL

HOLIDAY TRAINS AND EXCURSIONS

Holiday expresses, such as this one carrying Leicester workers and their families to the seaside, ran regularly – often on summer Saturdays – during the peak season and most large cities possessed their own headboards for attaching to the locomotive, which in this case is ex-LMS Stanier 5MT No. 45263. RAIL PHOTOPRINTS

Returning its passengers back to reality after a week of holiday-camp fun at Skegness is B1 No. 61179, heading south through Stevenage with the 'Butlin's Express' in June 1962. The loco is carrying the Great Northern version of Butlin's headboard. Trains from Liverpool Street to Butlin's Clacton camp carried headboards that didn't contain an apostrophe 's'. JOHN CHALCRAFT

TRAINS have long been associated with holidays and a number of dedicated services have been run over the years to various resorts or holiday camps.

Some, such as the 'Sunny South Express' and the 'Golden Sands Express', ran to regular timings and are thus included in the main directory, but most excursion trains were not fully timetabled and were usually run on an irregular basis in connection with a specific venue, such as a holiday camp or beach resort. Among them can be included:

- BARROW-IN-FURNESS HOLIDAY EXPRESS
- BUTLIN EXPRESS / BUTLIN'S EXPRESS *
- CITY OF BIRMINGHAM HOLIDAY EXPRESS
- CITY OF BRISTOL HOLIDAY EXPRESS
- THE CITY OF LEICESTER HOLIDAY EXPRESS
- CITY OF PLYMOUTH HOLIDAY EXPRESS
- CORNISH HOLIDAYMAKER
- DORSET HOLIDAYMAKER
- EASTERN BELLE +
- GLOUCESTERSHIRE HOLIDAY EXPRESS
- HOLIDAY CAMPS EXPRESS **
- HOLIDAYMAKER SHUTTLE
- INTERCITY HOLIDAYMAKER
- PEMBROKE COAST HOLIDAY EXPRESS
- SHEFFIELD SEASIDE EXPRESS
- SOMERSET & WILTS HOLIDAY EXPRESS
- SOUTH WALES HOLIDAYMAKER
- SPRING FAIR EXPRESS (London-Birmingham Int)
- SWANSEA & DISTRICT HOLIDAY EXPRESS
- TORBAY HOLIDAYMAKER ***
- WEST COUNTRY HOLIDAY EXPRESS
- WEST MIDLANDS HOLIDAY EXPRESS
- WEYMOUTH SAND & CYCLE EXPLORER
- WINTER SPORTS EXPRESS ++
- WREXHAM HOLIDAY EXPRESS

* King's Cross-Skegness trains had curved headboards stating 'Butlins Express' (some were painted yellow). Liverpool Street-Clacton

trains had circular boards spelt 'Butlin Express'.

** 'Holiday Camps Expresses' ran from Liverpool Street to a variety of locations, including Gorleston and Caister-on-Sea. Four trains were run each Saturday from May to September: three via the East Suffolk Line to Lowestoft, reversing there to call at each of the stations to Gorleston, thus serving several holiday camps.

Motive power was mostly B17s to Lowestoft, thence D16s. Calling patterns varied; most ran non-stop Lowestoft or Oulton Broad South to Ipswich. The fastest journey was the 3pm ex-Liverpool Street, booked non-stop to Lowestoft, due 5.30 .

The fourth train had a totally different route, as the destination was holiday camps of the Norfolk coast. Normally leaving Liverpool Street at 10.50, it ran via Cambridge to the Wensum Curve, Norwich, where engines were changed, to call at Wroxham, then to Antingham Road Junction, just north of North Walsham. There the front engine was uncoupled, but assisted for several yards, at what was now the rear, for the difficult start on the 1-in-73. The fresh engine, regularly a vacuum-fitted J17 would work tender-first. After passing through North Walsham Town, the J17 ambled eastwards along the M&GN, stopping at Potter Heigham, then Hemsby (at both of which drawing-up was necessary), then Caister Camp Halt, and finally Caister-on-Sea, at 3.22pm.

*** A Glasgow-Paignton overnight train active in the mid-1980s.

+ The case of the 'EASTERN BELLE' is an odd one. This Pullman train was launched in summer 1929 and unusually ran as a half-day or full-day excursion from London Liverpool Street to a different resort each day, thereby following no set itinerary. Among its various destinations were Felixstowe, Aldeburgh, Frinton, Yarmouth, Cromer, Hunstanton and even as far afield as Skegness. On Sundays, however, it almost always ran to Clacton-on-Sea and gained a separate title and headboard – the 'Clacton Belle' (sometimes known as the 'Clacton Sunday Pullman'). It is this regularity that earns the Clacton working an entry in the main text.

++ The Winter Sports Express was run by the Southern Railway and left Victoria at 2pm (via Calais) or 4.20pm (via Boulogne), taking wealthy skiiers to the Kent ports to catch ferries to Europe.

LEEDS BRADFORD & MORECAMBE RESIDENTIAL EXPRESS

THE concept of 'residential trains' was developed in the early part of the 20th century and enabled wealthy industrialists and their families to live long distances from their workplaces. Nowhere was this more graphically illustrated than on the Lancashire coast at Morecambe, which began to be known as "Bradford-by-the-Sea".

The fact that the Midland Railway had a direct route from the West Riding to Morecambe made it easier to travel there than to larger resorts such as Blackpool – and the 'Leeds, Bradford & Morecambe Residential Express' (sometimes informally known as the 'Midland Railway Club Train') became something of an institution in the area, also enabling shopfloor workers to flock to the coast for day trips and holidays.

It usually ran to and from Morecambe Promenade station.

the Lake District between Carnforth and Carlisle (to Windermere) but in 1927 there was also a line to Keswick.

'The Lakes Express', which was inaugurated on July 11 that year, served both those towns by splitting into portions. Departure from Euston was noon and after stopping at Wigan (to drop off coaches for Blackpool) and Preston (to detach a Barrow section), it was into Oxenholme at 4.48pm to divide the train.

The section for Keswick and Workington continued on its way north, while a 4-4-2T or 4-6-2T branch line loco ambled down into the valley to Kendal and Windermere with the main part of the train.

The Workington portion, though, may have made titled train history between the wars, as severe bridge restrictions on the former Cockermouth, Keswick & Penrith line meant haulage along that section by a veteran Webb 'Cauliflower' 0-6-0... possibly one of the smallest engines ever to handle a titled train.

The war brought the usual curtailment and it was June 5, 1950, before the train revelled once more in its title. But it had gone again by the end of August 1972.

Today, Keswick has no train service at all but Windermere is served well by Trans-Pennine.

THE LANCASTRIAN

THIS was one of many named trains discontinued at the outbreak of war but resurrected by the nationalised BR in the 1950s. 'The Lancastrian' was originally instigated on February 1, 1928 and ran as the 6pm Euston to Manchester London Road and midday return. Before the war, the train was unusual in that its southbound working not only took a different route to the down train, but it had to be diagrammed for different motive power too, for 'Royal Scots' and Pacifics were too heavy to work over the Stoke-on-Trent route and had to be replaced by a 'Jubilee' or 'Patriot', which usually required banking assistance in the Macclesfield area. The train was a mirror image of 'The Mancunian', which travelled via Stoke in the down direction.

The 'Lancastrian was discontinued when war broke out and although an approximate descendants of it could be found in the timetable, it wasn't until September 16, 1957 that the name was formally relaunched – and then it was for a different train, the 7.55 from Euston and the 4pm return.

Between April and September 1960, the train was diverted into Manchester Exchange during the building of London Road and its final run as a titled train was on September 8, 1962 before electrification work saw many expresses switched temporarily to the ex-Midland route.

In 2000, Virgin Trains revived the title for a Preston-Euston service (up direction only), extended to Carlisle in 2001.

LEEDS EXECUTIVE

IN common with the 'Bradford Executive' and 'Newcastle Executive', this train was introduced in 1971 and officially named two years later. Loco-hauled, it ran from King's Cross to Leeds and Harrogate and was eventually eclipsed by the arrival of 125mph HSTs on the East Coast Main Line. It disappeared from the timetable in May 1986.

THE LEWISMAN

THE remote location of Kyle of Lochalsh was graced with not one, but two named trains.

'The Lewisman' was an LMS train that departed from the Kyle, with a through coach for Glasgow in its formation, at 5.05 on a summer's morning, and arrived in Inverness at 8.10am. In the passing loop at Achnasheen, it would have encountered its sister train, 'The Hebridean'.

Two hours after arriving in Inverness, 'The Lewisman', having acquired a restaurant car, set off at 10.15 for the Kyle and finished its day there at 1.40pm.

In winter months, only two of those four workings operated, which meant the restaurant car being swapped over from one train to the other each time they got to Achnasheen.

'The Lewisman' was withdrawn when war broke out and never revived.

'LIMITED MAIL'

MANY overnight trains in other parts of the world have carried both mail vans and sleeping cars, but in Britain the two have largely remained separate. An exception was this train, which was introduced by the LNWR on the West Coast Main Line in the 1880s and ran from London Euston to Glasgow Central. It is not known when it ceased to be a mixed service.

(The South Eastern Railway is known to have

THE LANCASHIRE PULLMAN

A TITLE applied to the 16.45 Euston-Blackpool North train from 1984. By winter '93/94, the destination was Lancaster and in summer 1994, it changed to Carlisle (16.40 ex-Euston), with an up service at 05.38 from the Border city. The name had been dropped by summer 1998, although trains continued to run in the same time slots for a while.

(THE) LOTHIAN COAST EXPRESS

A SISTER to 'The Fife Coast Express', this summers-only train was operated by the North British Railway from June 1912 to September 1922 (with a break during the First World War) and by the LNER from June 1923 to September 1934, when it was discontinued.

Its route was from Glasgow Queen Street to North Berwick via Edinburgh Waverley, with portions for Dunbar and (until 1932) Gullane.

The North British Railway led the field when it came to locomotive headboards, introducing them circa 1912. Until then, names on trains had been carried on carriage roofboards or not at all. Reid 4-4-0 No. 359 *Dirk Hatteraick* (later to become BR D29 No. 62412) waits to leave North Berwick. NRM

sometimes used the term 'Limited Mail' as an alternative to 'Club Train'.)

LIVERPOOL EXECUTIVE
ONE of several BR InterCity 'Executive' services, this one was introduced between Euston and Liverpool Lime Street in 1984, but lasted only a year (see next entry).

LIVERPOOL PULLMAN
COMPLETION of the West Coast electrification scheme in 1966 allowed the LMR to introduce all-new electric loco-hauled stock for 'Manchester Pullman' and 'Liverpool Pullman' services.

With a smaller London clientele, the 'Liverpool Pullman' did not justify a full Pullman coaching set, so four carriages were used, marshalled with four standard 2nd class vehicles. Two trains a day were operated, one leaving Euston for Liverpool Lime Street at 7.45am and an evening service at 6.10pm. Coming south, the departure times were 7.55am and 5.40pm.

Although at one time the fastest-ever start-to-stop regular timing in the UK, the train did not prove as successful as its Manchester counterpart and the title fell out of use in the autumn of 1974. A similar service, entitled 'The Liverpool Executive', was briefly resurrected in 1984 for a Euston-Lime Street service but lasted only a year before being replaced by the 'Merseyside Pullman'.

■ In LNWR days, Lime Street and Euston had been connected by a 'Liverpool Dining Car Express', but this is thought to have been a train description, not a title.

THE LOCHABER
ALTHOUGH preservation era trains are not included in this register, an exception has been made for 'The Lochaber' (and its predecessor 'The West Highlander' and successor 'The Jacobite'), as, together, they have been running to a regular timetable on a main line route for more than a quarter of a century. The summer-only service began

running on the West Highland line in 1984 and this year's timings see it leave Fort William at 10.15 with an extra high-season only service at 14.30.

LONDON-FISHGUARD CAR-CARRIER
ONE of several British Rail mixed passenger and car-carrying trains that ran from a dedicated terminal at Kensington Olympia in the 1970s. This one was headboarded for a while and ran on Western Region metals to take passengers and their vehicles to Fishguard Harbour, in south-west Wales. It was also known as the 'London Irish Car Carrier'.

THE LORD OF THE ISLES
A NAME given in 1989 to the 06.52 Class 156-operated DMU from Edinburgh Waverley, which as two 2-car sets, split at Crianlarich, with one portion running to Oban, the other through to Mallaig via Fort William. It returned as the 18.22 ex-Mallaig and 20.32 from Oban.

The Mallaig service called at 29 stations and was unusual for a titled train in that it made request stops – at Locheilside and Beasdale. The title was dropped in 1991.

THE LORELEY
NAMED after a rock on the eastern bank of the River Rhine in Germany, 'The Loreley' was the name of a service that ran from Harwich Parkeston Quay to Blackpool in the late 1980s.

The service was a combination of two previous named trains – 'The North-West Dane' and 'The Rhinelander', both of which had been discontinued in May 1988. Northbound, it left Harwich at 07.57 and in the southbound direction it set out as two trains (the 14.14 Blackpool North-Harwich and the 16.16 Birmingham New Street), both of which were merged into one at Peterborough.

It continued until 1991/92 (although latterly with window labels bearing the name 'Loreley Express') before being renamed the 'Vincent van Gogh'.

Right: In the frequent
absence of headboards
after the end of steam, the
appearance of the rolling
stock was often the only
way a titled train could be
identified from the lineside
– and the silver & blue
coaches of the 'Manchester
Pullman' were among the
most recognisable in the
country. The down train is
pictured near North
Bridge, Staffs. (In the inset,
note how the Pullman
emblem has been
redesigned to a more
stretched shape).
HUGH BALLANTYNE

Manchester Pullman

MANCHESTER EXPRESS

IN the pre-Grouping era, the London & North Western Railway had a 'Manchester Express' from Euston, while the Midland Railway competed over its own route from St Pancras with a 'Manchester Corridor Express'.

MANCHESTER PULLMAN

THERE were two distinct trains of this name, one on the East Coast and one on the West. On April 1, 1925, the LNER began running a 'London-Sheffield-Manchester Pullman' between King's Cross and Manchester Central via Retford. This was shortened to 'Manchester Pullman', but its life proved to be extremely short too and it was withdrawn after just five months, on September 19, 1925.

The second manifestation of the train was far more successful: The wholesale electrification of the West Coast Main Line in the early 1960s saw almost all the steam-age named trains swept away, but the London Midland Region was keen to retain a special service for its valued first class Manchester-London customers and so launched an all-new train with purpose-built rolling stock. 'The

Manchester Pullman' made its entry in April 1966 and represented a departure from the norm in Pullman terms insofar as the traditional umber & cream livery of such coaches had been replaced by Mk 2s finished in a pearl grey & blue livery.

There were two eight-car sets designed to be hauled by AC electric locomotives and, at a stroke, they knocked a huge 40 minutes off the schedule of the diesel-operated 'Blue Pullmans' they replaced (although those had been travelling to St Pancras via the Midland Main Line).

The 'Manchester Pullman' diagram was extended in April 1967, allowing departures from Euston at 7.50am, 10.50am and 6pm. In May 1985, the Mk 2 stock was replaced with Mk 3s and non-Pullman standard-class coaches were also added. This was part of a revival of the Pullman brand by InterCity, with Merseyside and Yorkshire services being launched the same day.

The train became the last regular Pullman service on British Rail, not being withdrawn until the Virgin Trains era of the late-1990s.

Right: A fine study of
'Jubilee' 4-6-0 No. 45553
Canada working 'The
Mancunian' southwards
at Tring on April 12,
1952.RM ARCHIVE

Above: One of the few named expresses to use London Charing Cross station on a regular basis was 'The Man of Kent'. In this fine high-elevation view from the upper windows of Waterloo terminus in July 1959, the train is seen leaving the station (visible in the left background) behind Bulleid Pacific No. 34021 *Dartmoor* and is about to run through the platforms of Waterloo East on its way to Ramsgate. COLOUR-RAIL

THE MANCUNIAN

AN observer spending a day by the side of the West Coast Main Line in the late-1950s could have witnessed a veritable procession of headboarded trains – five of which would have started with the letter 'M'.

'The Mancunian' was one of that quintet, the others being 'The Manxman', the 'Merseyside Express', 'The Mid-Day Scot' and 'The Midlander'.

'The Mancunian', as the name implies, started from Manchester and had been launched by the LMS on September 26, 1927. It started each day as two portions (one containing coaches from Colne, Huddersfield and Rochdale) which were joined at Wilmslow before making a direct run to Euston at more than a mile a minute behind a Pacific or 'Royal Scot'.

In the reverse direction, however, the train's route became a mirror image of that of 'The Lancastrian' and had to be hauled by a 'Patriot' or 'Jubilee' due to being routed via the weight-limited Stoke-on-Trent line.

The 'Mancunian was discontinued when war broke out but on September 26, 1949, the name was returned to the 9.45am from Manchester and 6pm return.

Between April and September 1960, the train was diverted into Manchester Exchange station during the rebuilding of London Road. It was finally abandoned altogether as a named train on April 15, 1966, as electrics took over the workings on the West Coast Main Line.

THE MAN OF KENT

'THE Man of Kent' was one of the few named trains to use London Charing Cross. Pre-war, an un-named service had left that station at 4.15pm for Folkestone, Dover, Deal and Ramsgate and in 1953, BR Southern Region decided to reinstate it and honour it with a title.

The service had traditionally been worked by 'Schools' 4-4-0s or Light Pacifics, but electrification of the route saw the twice-daily train replaced by an hourly service and its final run was made on June 10, 1961.

THE MANXMAN

THIS train took its name from the term used to describe a resident of the Isle of Man and operated in summer only. It ran from Euston to Liverpool Lime Street to enable passengers to catch Isle of Man ferries sailing from Liverpool pier head.

It commenced operations on July 11, 1927 and was unusual in that it contained through coaches for Swansea, those being detached at Stafford and worked through to their South Wales destination via Shrewsbury on a very roundabout route that saw them arrive in Swansea Victoria at 6.35pm – more than four hours after the main part of the train had reached Liverpool.

Reintroduced after the war, this popular train resumed operations as a titled train on July 2, 1951 and continued until falling victim to the new all-electric timetable of 1966.

Against the very grimy metalwork of Stanier Pacific No. 46203 *Princess Margaret Rose*, the red headboard of 'The Manxman' stands out more than usual in this 1960s view. COLOUR-RAIL

THE MARY ROSE

NAMED after a 16th century battleship salvaged in 1982 and preserved in Portsmouth harbour, this service was introduced by Network SouthEast in 1989/90. Formed of a Class 442 'Wessex' unit, it ran between Waterloo and Portsmouth but had sunk from the timetable by summer 1992.

THE MAYFLOWER *

IN the period between 1955 and 1957, a spate of train namings took place on the Western Region in conjunction with a reprise of Great Western-style umber & cream rolling stock. Among them was the 8.30am Paddington-Plymouth North Road and 5.30pm return, upon which was bestowed the title 'The Mayflower' – the name of the ship upon which the Pilgrim Fathers had sailed from Plymouth to America in 1620.

'The Mayflower' was a restaurant car service calling at Taunton, Exeter, Newton Abbot and Plymouth with through coaches to Torquay, Paignton, Kingswear and

THE MASTER CUTLER *

COMPARED with the East and West Coast Main Lines, the former Great Central route from London Marylebone to Sheffield was very poorly served by titled trains, but one of the two it did possess was something of a celebrity.

Its unusual name was derived from the title of a ceremonial post in the city of Sheffield, which at the time was Britain's steel centre and supplied cutlery to the world.

There had been a 7.30am up breakfast train during LNER days, but the 'Cutler' wasn't formally christened until the very last days of that company, on October 6, 1947, so spent most of its titled existence under the auspices of BR.

It was noteworthy for another reason, insofar as it used no fewer than three London termini over the years, none of which were for diversionary reasons.

The first route was the time-honoured one from Marylebone to Sheffield Victoria and the timings were improved in the mid-1950s when Gresley A3 Pacifics were drafted in from the East Coast Main Line for a few years.

Once those locos had returned to the GN section, BR decided that a city the size of Sheffield should have its own Pullman service and that it should take 'The Master Cutler' name. The old train ceased to run on September 13, 1958 and, two days later, the new one was launched into service – but from King's Cross, not Marylebone.

This meant that the timings could be speeded up, especially as the train could benefit from the new English Electric Type 4 diesels that were arriving on the ECML at that time and which were diagrammed to the new six-car Pullman rake.

Leaving Sheffield Victoria at 7.20am and arriving in the capital at 10.05am, the set was not left idle all day but sent back to Sheffield on a 2hr 55min return trip, arriving back in London ready for a 7.20pm departure. For this middle of the day infill turn, the 'Master Cutler' title was dropped and the train became the 'Sheffield Pullman'.

Although Victoria station in Sheffield had another five years of life left in it, the 'Cutler' was transferred away to the neighbouring Midland station in October 1965 and then, in October 1968, was transferred to the London Midland Region and began operating out of St Pancras, its third London starting point, as a non-Pullman service.

At first it was as an anonymous 7.20am from Sheffield and 5.50pm return (meaning that technically the 'Master Cutler' had been discontinued), but from January 6, 1969, the name – and even some of the original headboards – were returned to the train and it continued to run as 'The Master Cutler' until May 10, 1985 when HSTs took over some of the services on the Midland main line. After a gap of some 18 months, the title (this time as 'Master Cutler Pullman') reappeared, in timetables only, and continued for the best part of the next decade. During this period, it was noteworthy for several years in being the only passenger train to run non-stop through Leicester station.

A service of the same name was resurrected in the Privatisation era and today runs as East Midlands Trains' 07.27 up and 16.55 down (Mon-Fri).

* As an interesting footnote, some of the headboards carried by the train in the 1950s were made in Sheffield of stainless steel and presented to BR by the manufacturers.

Right: An early British Railways pamphlet from September 1948 promoting 'The Master Cutler' restaurant car train and showing its route along the ex-Great Central main line from London Marylebone to Sheffield Victoria.

Below: The transfer of 'The Master Cutler' Pullman from the Great Central to Great Northern routes in 1958 coincided with the introduction that year of the 2,000hp English Electric Type 4s. In this official photograph, ex-works No. D207 is seen with the headboard, which was embellished with the arms of the Company of Cutlers on one side and those of the City of Sheffield on the other.

From the publishers of *The Railway Magazine*

Venturer' identity was bestowed upon the 11.15am from Paddington to Bristol and 5.25pm return and began running as a named train on the day the festival opened – May 3, 1951 – continuing beyond Bristol to serve the Somerset resort of Weston-super-Mare.

A through portion for Taunton was initially detached at Bristol, but that part of the operation was soon discontinued. The main train continued to run for more than 10 years, well into the diesel era, and didn't lose its identity until September 9, 1961.

The train – which takes its name from the Society of Merchant Venturers, an organisation established in Bristol since 1552 – was revived between 1983 and 1985 and then again in 2010, running today as the 07.30 Paddington-Bristol-Penzance. There is a 16.00 up service but it starts from Bristol.

THE MERSEYSIDE EXPRESS
See next page

Above: Changes in the design of headboards through the decades were relatively frequent, especially in BR days. In this engine-changing scene at Bristol Temple Meads, the Western Region's plaque, featuring the Bristol city coat of arms, can be compared directly with the more utilitarian BR standard style, which is depicted again in the lower photo attached to prototype gas-turbine locomotive No.18100. RAIL PHOTOPRINTS

Truro. Its inaugural run took place on June 17, 1957 and it was withdrawn on June 12, 1965, although briefly reinstated between May 1970 and April 1971 to mark the 350th anniversary of the original ship's sailing.

It surfaced again between 1983 and 1985, was relaunched in 1998 and currently runs as FGW's 11.06 Paddington-Plymouth and 15.00 return.

THE MERCHANT VENTURER *

THIS was one of two titles (the other was 'The William Shakespeare') introduced by the Western Region of BR to mark the Festival of Britain in 1951. 'The Merchant

THE MERSEYSIDE PULLMAN

THIS name appeared in the mid 1980s, replacing the 'Liverpool Executive', and was applied to the 07.50 Euston-Liverpool and 07.10 return. Although partly Pullman, it was not a non-stop service and called at several intermediate stations. The title was dropped during the early part of the Virgin West Coast franchise in 1998 and officially ceased to exist in 2001.

THE MERSEYSIDER

A SHORT-lived Virgin Trains service between London Euston and Liverpool Lime Street, active between 2000 and 2002.

Right: Well over half a century after it was built, the pioneer *Deltic* still cuts an impressively modern sight. Here the 3,300hp English Electric prototype is at Halton Junction, south of Runcorn, heading from Liverpool Lime Street to London Euston with 'The Merseyside Express' in June 1957. RAIL PHOTOPRINTS

Below: Skimming over Castlethorpe water troughs on its way to London is 'Princess Royal 4-6-2 No. 46207 *Princess Arthur of Connaught* with a heavily-loaded 'Merseyside Express' in August 1958. COLOUR-RAIL

THE MERSEYSIDE EXPRESS

ORIGINALLY known as 'The London and Merseyside Express', a title conferred by the LMS on September 26, 1927, this train had its name shortened on March 1, 1928 and continued to run until September 1939 when the war brought a temporary end to the proceedings.

It linked Liverpool Lime Street with London Euston and included a Southport Chapel Street portion, which was originally attached at Edge Hill, later Lime Street.

After the war, the train was reintroduced by BR on September 26, 1949, and hit the headlines on December 12, 1955 when English Electric's blue-liveried prototype *Deltic* made its debut on the up 'Merseyside Express', going on to haul many trains on the West and East Coast Main lines over the next five years.

As with so many other West Coast titled trains, the express met its demise in the great timetable speed-up of 1966, its last run being on April 16.

Left: No. 46207, cleaner than when seen on the facing page, thunders through the north London suburbs with 'The Mid-Day Scot' in September 1961.
COLOUR-RAIL

THE MID-DAY SCOT

ALTHOUGH this train had been running since 1889 and had been affectionately known by staff and regular passengers as "The Corridor", it was not until September 1927 that the 'Mid-Day Scot' title was officially conferred.

The earlier (unofficial) name referred to the equipping of the train with the then-new corridor stock throughout in the summer of 1893. Until 1932, its timings had been artificially restrained by an agreement between the West and East Coast companies not to undercut each other by running Anglo-Scottish trains in less than 8¼ hours, but after the end

of that bond in 1932, the schedule of 'The Mid-Day Scot', along with those of all other expresses, began to be dramatically reduced.

It was a train that, over the years, included various portions in its formation, including through coaches for places like Blackpool, Stranraer, Edinburgh and Aberdeen.

The train officially lost its name upon the outbreak of war, but was so important to the operation of the West Coast Main Line that it continued to run, on and off, throughout the hostilities. Formally given back its identity in September 1949, it was a regular preserve of Pacific locos until the title was removed from the timetable on June 13, 1965.

With its lamps and firebox glow piercing the dusk at Darlaston, West Midlands, 'Jubilee' No. 45738 *Samson* charges through with 'The Midlander' (see next page for text).
Painting by GERALD BROOM

THE MIDLANDER

'THIS was one of the quintet of West Coast expresses
beginning with 'M' and was a product of the London Midland
Region of BR as it strove to create an identity for itself in the
early months of Nationalisation.

The title was conferred upon the 9.45am
Wolverhampton-Euston (which travelled via the
Northampton loop) and the 5.45pm return, which began
running as a titled train on September 25, 1950, more
often than not behind a 'Jubilee' 4-6-0.

Three years later, the timetable was recast and 'The
Midlander' became an 11am ex-Wolverhampton and a
5.30pm from Euston, continuing until September 11,
1959 when the name was dropped from everyday use,
although it didn't officially cease to exist until the great
London Midland Region purge of 1966.

MIDLAND PULLMAN

**Right station, wrong train: The
'Midland Pullman' after arrival
at Manchester Piccadilly – but
the 'Blue Pullman' set depicted
here is actually one of the
eight-car Western Region fleet.
The correct six-car version is
depicted (right) at St Pancras
(the wording on the side being
a way of telling them apart).**
RAIL PHOTOPRINTS

**THE temporary upheaval caused by the West Coast electrification project in the
early-1960s threatened to harm the lucrative first class business traffic between
Manchester and London so, in 1960, the London Midland Region laid on a first class
only high-speed alternative via its ex-Midland Millers Dale route to London St
Pancras.**

**This 'Midland Pullman' was a 'Blue Pullman' service similar to those introduced
onto the Western Region (see 'Birmingham Pullman') and worked out of Manchester
Central. Launched in July 1960, the two semi-streamlined six-car Metro-Cammell
DMUs raced from London to Manchester in 3hr 15min, slicing more than half an
hour off the previous Midland line best.**

**Instead of lying dormant in London during the day, one of the sets was used for
an out-and-back infill turn as far as Leicester and Nottingham.**

**The service was withdrawn in 1966 when the modernised West Coast route was
restored to full use; the Derby-Manchester line later being closed as a through route.**

The
Midland Scot
Birmingham — Glasgow

MIDLAND SCOT

A NAME applied by British Rail InterCity to a Birmingham
New Street-Glasgow return service in the 1970s. The title
was dropped in 1983/84 but returned in the winter of 1991
and was continued by franchise holder Virgin Trains until
1998/99.

MIDLANDS EXPRESS

AN HST-formed service that was introduced by the Midland
Mainline TOC between London St Pancras and Sheffield in
1999.

Originally bearing the slightly different name 'Midland
Express', it left Sheffield at 07.05 and was latterly
operated by East Midlands Trains. Its last day of operation
was December 12, 2008, by which time it had also been
worked by Class 170 'Turbostars' and Class 222
'Meridians'.

THE MORNING CALEDONIAN

IN 1958, the frequency of the West Coast express 'The
Caledonian' was doubled and in the summer of that year,
'The Morning Caledonian' and 'The Afternoon Caledonian'
were in operation, although the wording on the locomotive
headboards remained unchanged. 'The Morning
Caledonian' left Euston at 7.45am.

THE MORNING TALISMAN

BR doubled the frequency of the East Coast express 'The
Talisman' in 1957 and, for that summer and the duration of
the September 1958 to June 1959 timetable, the services
were referred to in timetables as 'The Morning Talisman' and
'The Afternoon Talisman', although the original loco
headboards continued to be used. Departure time from
King's Cross for 'The Morning Talisman' was 7.45am and
from Edinburgh 8.30am.

The reason for the gap in the timetable was that from
September 1957 to September 1958, the 'Morning
Talisman' ran under the title 'The Fair Maid'.

THE MOTORAIL LIMITED

A EUSTON-Stirling car-carrying train active in 1983. All other
such services around the country were by then being
collectively operated under the plain 'Motorail' brand and
therefore didn't have individual train names.

FAMOUS INTERNATIONAL NAMED TRAINS - A SELECTION

ALTHOUGH only one country (the United States of America) has had more titled trains than Great Britain, there have been many hundreds of named services overseas and still are, especially in India. The following is a small selection of the more notable foreign services, both past and present. Please note that the list includes brands (e.g. Shinkansen, Hiawatha, Talgo) as well as individual names.

- American Royal Zephyr (USA)
- Andean Explorer (Peru)
- Aztec Eagle (Mexico/USA)
- Bernina Express (Switzerland/Italy)
- Blue Train (South Africa)
- Brenner Express (Italy/Germany)
- Broadway Limited (USA)
- The Canadian (Canada)
- Danube Express (Hungary-Turkey/Poland)
- Deccan Queen Express (India)
- The Diplomat (USA)
- The Dominion (Canada)
- Eastern & Oriental Express (SE Asia)
- Empire Builder (USA)
- Étendard (France)
- Flèche d'Or (France)
- Flying Bluenose (Canada)

- The Ghan (Australia)
- Geyserland Express (New Zealand)
- Glacier Express (Switzerland)
- Golden Chariot (Indian land cruise)
- Golden Temple Mail (India)
- Hiawatha (USA)
- Hiram Bingham (Peru, tourist train)
- Indian Pacific (Australia)
- Karachi Express (Pakistan)
- Kingston Flyer (New Zealand)
- Khyber Mail (Pakistan)
- Leonardo da Vinci (Italy/Austria/Germany)
- Lone Star (USA)
- Michelangelo (Italy/Austria/Germany)
- Mistral (France)
- Moonlight Nagara (Japan)
- Newcastle Flyer (Australia)
- Nord Express (France plus others)
- Orient Express (France to Turkey)
- Overlander (New Zealand)
- Palace on Wheels (Indian tourist train)
- Pennsylvania Limited (USA)
- Picasso (Spain)
- Polar Bear Express (Canada)
- Prospector (Australia)
- Punjab Mail (India)

- Queen of the Oceans (Sri Lanka)
- Rheingold Express (Switz/Germany/Holland)
- Rocky Mountaineer (Canadian tourist train)
- Rossiya (Russia)
- Shinkansen (Japan)
- Silver Streak Zephyr (USA)
- Southern Belle (USA)
- Spirit of Progress (Australia)
- Sud Express (France/Spain/Portugal)
- Super Chief (USA)
- Super Continental (Canada)
- The Sunlander (Australia)
- Sunset Limited (USA)
- Talgo (Spain/France)
- Taj Express (India)
- Tequila Express (Mexico)
- Texas Chief (USA)
- Trail Blazer (USA)
- Train Bleu (France)
- TransAlpin (Switzerland/Austria)
- Trans-Karoo Express (South Africa)
- Trans-Siberian Express/Rossiya (Russia)
- TranzAlpine (New Zealand)
- 20th Century Limited (USA)
- Wabash Cannonball (USA)
- Zambezi Express (Zambia)

Top right: With a simple letter 'B' on its headboard sufficing to tell onlookers they are in the presence of a world-famous entity, South Africa's 'Blue Train' runs through Cape Town.
Top left: The observation car of America's '20th Century Limited'. This train inspired the name of Britain's '21st Century Limited'.
Left: The 'Eastern & Oriental Express' luxury tour train crosses the Bridge over the River Kwai in Thailand.
Right: France's 'Étendard' headboard on loco 6531. The name means 'The Flag'.

NEWCASTLE EXECUTIVE

IN common with the 'Bradford Executive' and 'Leeds Executive', this train was introduced in 1971 and officially named two years later. Locomotive-hauled, it left Newcastle at 07.40 and London at 17.30 but was eventually eclipsed by the arrival of 125mph HSTs on the ECML and had disappeared from the timetable by May 1986.

NEWCASTLE PULLMAN

A first-class express introduced by British Rail between King's Cross and Newcastle from 1991 to 2004.

THE NIGHT ABERDONIAN

THIS title was most unusual in describing trains that ran on both the East and West Coast main lines. Its initial manifestation was as an Aberdeen sleeping car service that left King's Cross at 10.15pm, making its first advertised stop at Inverkeithing, although also halting at Newcastle and Edinburgh for locomotive changes. Commencing in 1971, it continued until the title was dropped in October 1982. (See also 'The Aberdonian').

The West Coast version was introduced in 1989 and served Aberdeen until September 1996 when it became part of the 'Caledonian Sleeper' set-up.

THE NIGHT CALEDONIAN

THIS name describes two separate trains. One was a West Coast sleeper service from Euston to Glasgow between 1970 and 1976, being revived briefly between the late-1980s and 1996.

The second ran cross-country, linking Penzance/Bristol with Glasgow/Edinburgh and Aberdeen, but was fairly short-lived, being in operation in 1984/85.

THE NIGHT CAPITALS

A SLEEPING car train that ran on the East Coast route from King's Cross to Edinburgh and Perth between 1971 and 1979.

NIGHT LIMITED

A NEW name for the 'Night Scot' once the all-electric service had started on the southern part of the West Coast Main Line after 1966. The title was later used to describe a Euston-Glasgow train between 1982 and 1988/9.

(THE NIGHTRIDER)

(*Brand name*): Introduced on May 17, 1982, 'The Nightrider' name applied to overnight expresses from King's Cross to Scotland that offered non-sleeping car accommodation (i.e. seats) for heavily-discounted fares, yet ran with first class coaches only. It sounds a contradiction in terms, but the idea was to offer budget travellers a more comfortable alternative to cheap road coach travel.

The trains divided at Edinburgh with one portion going to Aberdeen and the other to Glasgow, arrival times being 8.31am and 7am respectively, while London-bound patrons pitched up in the capital at 6.37am. Occasionally, 'The Nightrider' brand applied not to a whole train but to the seated sections of certain sleeping car trains.

Between 1983 and 1990, a West Coast version ran between Euston and Glasgow Central, but the last runs on both routes were made in 1990.

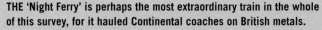

THE NIGHT FERRY

THE 'Night Ferry' is perhaps the most extraordinary train in the whole of this survey, for it hauled Continental coaches on British metals.

Such international operation became possible on the night of October 5, 1936, with the completion of train ferry terminals at Dover and Dunkirk, enabling a whole train to be shipped across the English Channel, complete with slumbering first class passengers!

The Wagons-Lits coaches were reduced to fit the British loading gauge, but, nevertheless, the sight of the dark blue French-built coaches in London's Victoria station every day was still a remarkable one – made the more remarkable by the fact that Customs checks had to be carried out at Victoria before anyone was allowed to alight.

The coaches, which were conveyed across the Channel by a Southern Railway-owned ferry (and which contained a lifebuoy in each carriage compartment!) ran for three years before the war intervened, but the service was resumed on December 15, 1947.

The 'Night Ferry' was one of the heaviest regular peacetime passenger workings in Britain, requiring 'Merchant Navy' Pacifics to be transferred to Dover shed to handle it. Even so, double-heading using a Light Pacific and a 4-4-0 as pilot was necessary whenever the train was booked to run via Canterbury East because of stiff gradients.

After 1958, Bo-Bo electric locomotives (later Class 71) took over, but, by the 1970s, the 1936 coaches were ageing and, with airlines having taken much of the train's clientele away, it was decided to put it out of its misery in 1980, the last train running on November 1.

By then, it had dwindled to just six or seven vehicles, including luggage vans. A sad end to a train that, in a way, had presaged the Channel Tunnel.

The Night Caledonian

Stonehaven – Montrose – Arbroath – Dundee – Leuchars – Cupar – Kirkcaldy – Inverkeithing – Edinburgh – Carstairs – Carlisle – Preston – Wigan – Crewe – Stafford – Wolverhampton – Birmingham New Street – Cheltenham – Bristol Parkway – Bristol Temple Meads – Exeter St. Davids – Plymouth – Bodmin Road – Par – St Austell – Truro – Redruth – Camborne – Hayle – St. Erth – Penzance

InterCity

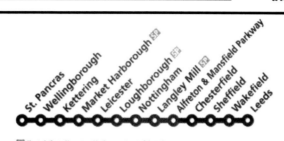

St. Pancras – Wellingborough – Kettering – Market Harborough – Leicester – Loughborough – Nottingham – Langley Mill – Alfreton & Mansfield Parkway – Chesterfield – Sheffield – Wakefield – Leeds

Short platform. Please travel in the correct part of the train.

STRATFORD-UPON-AVON

Oxford – Banbury – Leamington Spa –

Warwick

Stations shown in red have short platforms.
Passengers are advised to travel in the correct portion of the train.

Far left: The circular headboard of the 'Night Ferry' was one of the most eye-catching used in the UK on a regular basis. In this picture taken at Stewarts Lane shed, south London, on September 8, 1957, it is attached to unrebuilt 'Merchant Navy' No. 35001 *Channel Packet*. R C RILEY

Above: The only French-style passenger coaches to be seen running a British main line in steam days were those of the 'Night Ferry'. This is the up train near St Mary Cray Junction in May 1959, double-headed by L1 4-4-0 No, 31753 and 'Battle of Britain' No. 34087 *145 Squadron*. COLOUR-RAIL

Left: 'Night Ferry' stock being shunted into the hold of a cross Channel ferry. Once on the Continent, it was divided in order to serve Paris and Brussels.

Like its 'Caledonian' sleeping car cousin on the West Coast, the Great Western Main Line's 'Night Riviera' continues to run in the modern era. In the early morning of August 15, 2011, it is captured by the camera at Moorswater, Cornwall, behind Class 57 No. 57605 *Totnes Castle* as it nears journey's end at Penzance. RON WESTWATER

A British Rail brochure from the mid 1980s.

(THE) NIGHT RIVIERA *

BRITAIN currently has only three regular sleeping car services – two 'Caledonian Sleeper' trains out of Euston and the 'Night Riviera' from Paddington.

The latter, which has its origins in a broad gauge service of the 1870s, is operated by First Great Western and runs six days a week from London to Plymouth and Penzance, departing at a quarter to midnight with the London-bound train leaving the Cornish terminus at 21.45.

In the aftermath of a serious fire on board the train at Taunton in 1978, in which 12 passengers died, BR ordered modifications to Mk 3 sleeping cars that were already on order and gave the train a long-overdue official title – one that played heavily on the successful marketing strengths of the daytime 'Cornish Riviera Express'.

After using London Waterloo as its base for a while

between May 1995 and September 1998 in order to provide a connection with Eurostar passengers, 'The Night Riviera' went through a period in which patronage dropped to uneconomic levels on some nights (it had included the UK's last Motorail service but that was dropped in 2005 due to low usage). However, local campaigns in the West Country coupled with an upsurge in custom has seen it survive and today it provides a regular passenger diagram for a diesel loco, Class 57s being the normal motive power. Departure times on weekdays are Paddington (23.50) and Penzance (21.45), and on Sundays 23.45 and 21.15. There is no Saturday service.

For a while in 2007/08, the train's carriage destination labels bore the name 'The Night Riviera Sleeper'.

THE NIGHT SCOT

BETWEEN 1895 and 1932, the East and West Coast companies had an agreement not to cut the schedules of their Anglo-Scottish day trains to less than 8¼ hours, but there was no similar restriction on night trains, so the 'Night Scot' sleeping car train often completed its journeys between Euston and Glasgow anything up to half an hour faster.

A predecessor of today's 'Caledonian Sleepers', the train left Euston at around quarter to midnight and got its passengers to their Scottish destinations in good time for the next day. The up train left Glasgow at 10.45 and arrived in Euston at 7.15am.

With the onset of the Second World War, the name was dropped but the train itself remained and became longer

and heavier, with much of its accommodation reserved for troops. On numerous nights, even that wasn't enough and a number of relief trains had to be laid on. The wartime WCML in the wee small hours was an extremely busy line!

Strangely, given BR's penchant for naming trains in the 1950s, that appears to have been the very decade in which it was anonymous, but with electrification of the southern part of the West Coast route in the mid-1960s, a revised form of the train was created, bearing the name 'Night Limited', and that continued running into the 1980s.

Between 1993 and 1995, the 'Night Scot' title was dusted off and used by BR to describe a nocturnal cross-country service from Plymouth to Glasgow/Edinburgh.

THE NIGHT SCOTSMAN

ALTHOUGH incorporating half the name of its illustrious daytime equivalent, the 'Night Scotsman' was not nearly so well-known outside railway circles.

Its northbound service was christened officially on July 11, 1927 (with a headboard from 1932), but the corresponding up train had to wait until October 1946 before it was bestowed with the same title.

As with the West Coast's 'Night Scot', the train had been running since pre-Grouping days, departing King's Cross at 11.30 in the evening and taking eight hours to reach Edinburgh. So popular did it become with passengers to and from communities north of Edinburgh that, by the end of the 1930s, those wanting the Scottish capital itself were better off catching one of its relief trains!

The conveyance of portions to other towns and cities saw 'Night Scotsman' headboards carried by numerous modestly-sized steam locomotives in the Scottish provinces, often in broad daylight.

The main train (or at least the down part of it) was one of very few services to retain its title right through the Second World War and it carried vast amounts of custom during those difficult times. When peace returned, the LNER officially named the up service and made amends by also affixing roofboards to it.

Under BR control, the service was made non-stop between London and Newcastle but when sufficient 'Deltic' diesels were available to handle the train in the early 1960s, the journey time briefly plummeted to 6hrs 50mins before those responsible for night freight trains complained about pathing and the schedule was relaxed slightly.

The sleeping car train remained one of the few loco-

hauled trains on the King's Cross line well into the 1980s and even began hauling Motorail vans too, but today there are no overnight passenger services on the East Coast as they have been concentrated on the route out of Euston.

That major policy change brought about a situation that would have been considered unthinkable in pre-1948 days – a 'Night Scotsman' on the West Coast! Linking Euston and Edinburgh, the invader remained from 1987 until 1996.

Above: Nocturnal trains are, unsurprisingly, rare birds photographically, but this time-exposure made at King's Cross in 1937 has captured the headboard of the 'Night Scotsman'. The train at that time was only titled northbound, so although Gresley A1 No. 2548 *Galtee More* is at the buffer stops, it is thought to have been in the process of marshalling the stock. RAIL ARCHIVE STEPHENSON

SCOTLAND BY "THE NIGHT SCOTSMAN"
KING'S CROSS – DEPART 10·25 P.M.
FIRST AND THIRD CLASS SLEEPERS

Left: A dramatic interpretation of the train on a pre-war LNER poster.

Storming up the grade out of King's Cross with 'The Norseman' on June 29, 1953 is A4 No. 60003 *Andrew K McCosh*. The train would be carrying passengers to Newcastle's Tyne Commission Quay for onward travel to Norway by steamer. BRIAN MORRISON

THE NORSEMAN

THIS was a boat train service from King's Cross to Newcastle Tyne Commission Quay, introduced by the LNER on June 13, 1931, to connect with long-distance ferries to Bergen, in Norway (hence the title).

The war brought suspension in September 1939 and the immediate post-war service in 1946-47 was described as 'Norwegian Boat Express', but 'The Norseman' title was revived by BR on June 7, 1950, and one of the headboards carried during the BR era incorporated an image of a Viking longboat.

Pacific locomotives usually hauled the train along the East Coast Main Line, but came off at Newcastle to be replaced by tank engines for the trip down to the quay, making this one of the few named expresses in Britain to be hauled by tank engines as part of its regular diagram.

The last 'Norseman' ran on September 3, 1966, just 3½ years before ships stopped sailing from the Commission Quay.

The two Viking longboat motifs can be seen on each side of the headboard in this 1958 study of No. 60021 *Wild Swan* at King's Cross. COLOUR-RAIL

An immaculate *Britannia* waits for the right-away from London Liverpool Street with 'The Norfolkman' in the early 1950s. Painting by MALCOLM ROOT

NIGHT WEST COUNTRYMAN

A CROSS-country overnight train that ran from Glasgow and Edinburgh to Plymouth in the latter years of the British Rail era, 1992-95.

NORFOLK COAST EXPRESS

THIS was the title of a Great Eastern Railway service from Liverpool Street to Cromer between 1907 and 1914. It had been introduced in 1897 as the 'Cromer Express' and ran under that name until the change of title in 1907.

It was a corridor restaurant train that ran in summer only from London Liverpool Street to North Walsham in 2¼ hours, despite sometimes comprising as many as 14 coaches and being hauled by nothing more powerful than a 'Claud Hamilton' 4-4-0.

The operation of such a heavy train with the small engines of the day was a miracle of timekeeping, especially over grades such as the Bethnal Green and Brentwood banks.

At North Walsham, through coaches for Mundesley-on-Sea were detached and the train then continued to Cromer Jct, where coaches for Sheringham were dropped off, and finally ran into Cromer High with the main portion. Carriage roofboards proclaimed the train's name.

In the up direction, it left Cromer at 1pm and was back in Liverpool Street just before 4pm – timings that would be acceptable today, let alone before the First World War! The train ceased to run in 1914.

THE NORFOLKMAN

ONE of the first titled trains produced by the fledgling Eastern Region of British Railways was 'The Norfolkman', created in 1948 as a younger sister for 'The East Anglian'.

The latter left Norwich Thorpe at 11.40am and London Liverpool Street at 6.40pm and the new train was designed to provide similar facilities in the opposite direction, leaving the metropolis at 10am and returning at 5pm.

In summer, the service extended to Sheringham and Cromer, although the first summer was pretty much over by the time the train commenced operation on September 27. The Sheringham leg was later dropped.

Hauled at first by B1 4-6-0s, the trains had their schedules cut to 2hrs 10mins in 1951 to reflect the greater power of the new 'Britannia' Pacifics then being built and that same year, BR provided the service with brand new coaches.

From 1958, the train benefited yet again from shiny hardware when D200 and its fellow 2,000hp English Electric Type 4s began replacing steam on the GE section, but, just four years later, 'The Norfolkman' died on the same day as 'The Broadsman' and 'The East Anglian'.

The date was June 16, 1962 (a black day for titled trains but one that marked one of the biggest accelerations Britain's rail network has ever seen in one go.)

The title was resurrected in 1993 to describe the 08.00 Liverpool Street-Norwich service and continued as such until the summer of 2000.

NORMANDY EXPRESS

UNLIKE many south-western boat trains (page 27), this one did not run as an as-required 'Q train' to meet transatlantic voyages, but on a regular basis, running from London Waterloo to Southampton Docks thrice a week in connection with overnight ferry sailings between there and Le Havre, France. It was active from 1952 to 1964.

'NORMANDY BOAT EXPRESS'

A 1980s service from London Waterloo to the ferry terminal at Weymouth quay.

THE NORTH BRITON

THE majority of titled trains were London-centric. Even among the cross-country services, very few started in the middle of the British Isles and went north, but that's what the forerunner of 'The North Briton' did.

Inaugurated in the Edwardian era by the North Eastern Railway, its origination point was Leeds and it ran to Edinburgh via York and Newcastle, returning five hours later.

The idea behind the NER's decision was to try to persuade the people of the West Riding to use that 230-mile route to the Scottish capital rather than go via the Midland Railway's Leeds-Carlisle line, which was only 211 miles. In 1910, the NER extended the service to Glasgow and it was that service – the 8.48 from Leeds City and the 4pm from Glasgow Queen Street – that BR inherited and bestowed a formal title upon in September 1949.

The train became the very first in Britain to get back to a mile-a-minute schedule after the war and, in the mid-1960s, began to be further accelerated by Class 47 haulage, but, despite the improvements, it lost its name on May 4, 1968.

Fortunately, the anonymity lasted only four years, for the name was restored in 1972 and continued for a further three years.

'NORTH COUNTRY CONTINENTAL'

AN unofficial name, coined as far back as the Great Eastern Railway era of the 1880s, for the boat train from Harwich to the North, firstly to Doncaster and later to North-west England. This service has had more changes of identity than any other, having also been called at various times 'The European', 'The Rhinelander', 'The Loreley', the 'North-West Dane', the 'Vincent van Gogh' and (unofficially) the 'Harwich Boat Train', among others.

THE NORTH EASTERN

THIS East Coast express began running in 1904 but had to wait 60 years before its title was formalised. Leaving King's Cross at 5.30pm and reaching Tyneside by 10.42, it was jointly instigated by the Great Northern and North Eastern Railways and continued in roughly the same timings by the LNER and BR.

In 1963, the train was handed over to 'Deltic' haulage and the improvement was so great that in 1964 it was decided to name the train officially. Another leap forward came three years later when 'The North Eastern' was chosen to be one of the 'Deltic'-powered eight-coach flyers, which cut the time of the up train to 3hr 50min. The title was discontinued in 1968.

THE NORTH EXPRESS

THE Midland & South Western Junction Railway had two named trains – 'The North Express' and 'The South Express'. The latter was basically a 'mirror-image' of its northbound partner, which, in the half-decade prior to the First World War, ran from Southampton West to Cheltenham Lansdown via Andover Junction.

Although the 'South Express' continued after the conflict, its northbound cousin became anonymous.

THE NORTH-WEST DANE

ONE of several titles used to describe boat train services to Harwich Parkeston Quay over the years, this one was introduced in May 1987 as the 13.20 Harwich Parkeston

Above: A3 No. 60086 *Gainsborough,* of Leeds Neville Hill shed, prepares to leave Leeds City station with 'The North Briton' on March 25, 1961.
GAVIN MORRISON

Quay-Blackpool North with the corresponding service arriving back in Essex at 15.19. It was withdrawn in May 1988.

'(THE) NORTHERN BELLE'

See 'Land Cruise' trains panel on page 96.

THE NORTHERN IRISHMAN

NOT to be confused with 'The Irishman', this was a sleeping car train that ran between London Euston and Stranraer Harbour and carried a name from June 30, 1952 to April 17, 1966, losing it in the cull of West Coast titles that took place that month.

Prior to 1952, a train unofficially named the 'Stranraer Boat Express' (and nicknamed "The Paddy") had been running over the route and the new train continued to be referred to by the same sobriquet.

For all but the last 10 months of its existence as a named service, it ran via Dumfries and Newton Stewart, the tough gradients of the 'Port Road' frequently justifying use of 'Clan' Pacifics on the Carlisle-Stranraer section. After closure of the 'Port Road' line on June 14, 1965, the train had to travel via Ayr, adding a substantial 60 miles to the journey.

Sixteen years after that train's demise, the name was revived for a Euston-Stranraer service that operated from 1982 to 1985/6.

THE NORTHERN LIGHTS *

'THE Northern Lights' is one of East Coast's current HST services, departing King's Cross daily at 10.00 (including weekends) and running to Aberdeen, where it arrives at 17.09 (17.14 on Sundays). In the up direction, the name applies to the 09.52 Aberdeen-King's Cross (Mon-Sat) and the 09.47 Sundays-only train.

The train has caused some controversy as it has taken the time-honoured 10am departure slot, which for years had been the preserve of the 'Flying Scotsman' (the more famous title now being used only for an up service).The

'Northern Lights' name was first used for a King's Cross-Aberdeen service in the late-BR days of 1994.

THE NORTHUMBRIAN
WHILE some coaches of the 'Silver Jubilee' went off to join the 'Fife Coast Express' after the war, the triple articulated dining set was put to work on 'The Northumbrian'. This was a King's Cross-Newcastle lunchtime departure introduced by BR on September 26, 1949, although its down service had essentially been created by the LNER in May 1940 in order to prevent existing trains from growing too long to fit into station platforms. 'The Northumbrian' was a Pacific turn but set no speed or haulage records. It slipped quietly out of the timetables on June 13, 1964.

In 1988, the title was briefly revived by BR's CrossCountry sector to describe the 06.57 Newcastle-Poole and 12.03 reverse working. It disappeared again the following year.

NORWEGIAN BOAT EXPRESS
THE name of the LNER's King's Cross-Tyne Commission Quay service from 1928 to 1931 when it was renamed 'The Norseman'. Curiously, the old title briefly resurfaced in the timetable in 1946, possibly in error.

NOTTINGHAM EXECUTIVE
A SHORT-lived midweek Nottingham-London St Pancras HST service that ran in 1988/89, leaving the Midlands city at 07.40 but having no northbound named equivalent, due to the 18.15 down train continuing on to Sheffield.

NOTTINGHAM PULLMAN
INTRODUCED in May 1990, this was the 06.32 Sheffield-St Pancras via Nottingham (07.38) and 17.25 return (Nottingham 18.59). It ran for one summer only, being renamed 'The Robin Hood' at the beginning of October.

OBAN EXPLORER
THIS was a diesel multiple unit service that ran between Glasgow Queen Street and Oban in 1994 and carried titled train window labels. Literature was also published bearing the name 'Oban Express'.

OCEAN BOAT EXPRESS
REFERENCE has been found in a 1910 Baedeker's Guide to a train of this name running on the Midland & South Western Joint Railway (in addition to 'The North Express' and 'The South Express'). The 'Ocean Boat Express' is described as a Saturdays-only service running in the southbound direction from Cheltenham to Southampton Docks and appears to have been a through train from the North.

'OCEAN LINER EXPRESS'
AN unofficial name, thought to have been used by the London & South Western Railway for its Devonport-Waterloo passenger trains between 1903 and 1910. It is also possible that the name was used as a general term for Waterloo-Southampton deep sea boat trains before individual names began to be used. Another term used at the time was 'Ocean Special'.

THE ORCADIAN
THE first use of this name was in 1934, in connection with a pre-war LMS restaurant car train that left Wick for Inverness

at 3.30pm and returned the following morning.

The name was revived by BR in June 1962 to identify the 9.05am Inverness to Wick (and Thurso) and the 1.15pm return. The first working of the new service took place on June 29 and the train remained in the timetable only until September 5, 1964. Because steam disappeared from the Far North workings in 1961, the revived service is thought never to have been steam-hauled.

In the early 1980s, the title was reinstated again and applied to the 07.02 Inverness-Thurso and 11.40 return, the last timetabled use of the name being in 1991.

OXFORD PULLMAN
A SHORT-lived 'Blue Pullman' diesel service introduced in 1967. It left Paddington at 12.15pm and made a one-hour run to Oxford, arriving back in the capital, after a three-hour layover in the university city, at 5.15.

The service had been intended to attract American tourists to the delights of Oxford's 'dreaming spires', but did not prove a commercial success and was discontinued after just two years.

THE PALATINE
THE Midland route from London St Pancras couldn't boast anything like as many titled trains as its Euston neighbour, but in 1938 the LMS granted two of its Manchester services appropriate recognition. One was the 10am from Manchester Central and 4.30pm return, which was named

'The Palatine', and the other the 4.25pm and 10.30am versions of the same itinerary (see 'The Peak Express').

After being suspended for the duration of the war, 'The Palatine' (but not its sister) was resurrected on September 16, 1957, for the 7.55am from St Pancras and the 2.25pm from Manchester. The title was withdrawn in 1964, the last run being on June 13, and the scenic central part of the route over the Peaks is itself now a memory.

THE PARIS MAIL LIMITED

THIS was a 'train deluxe' introduced by the London, Chatham & Dover Railway in 1889 to connect with a Channel sailing at Dover for onward travel to Paris. It left London Victoria mid-afternoon. A rival South Eastern Railway train is understood to have run non-stop to Dover from Charing Cross. Both were nicknamed "Continental Club Trains" by the public.

THE PARISIENNE

THIS service was introduced by British Rail's Southern Region in 1983 and ran from London Waterloo to Portsmouth Harbour, for overnight ferry connections to northern France.

Although using Portsmouth rather than the Kent ports, it acted as a form of stop-gap between the demise of the 'Night Ferry' (which had ceased to run in 1980) and the opening of the Channel Tunnel (in 1994).

Operated by South Western Division electric multiple units, the service was perpetuated after 1986 by BR's Network SouthEast sector, which printed its own carriage destination labels in 1987. By May of that year, however, the service was being promoted by InterCity Europe in conjunction with Townsend Thorensen ferries.

PEAK DISTRICT PULLMAN

A FEW titled trains were virtually anonymous in that they carried no form of identification whatsoever on the train or even in timetables, the only clue to their name being printed on advertising leaflets!

Such an oddity was the 'Peak District Pullman', an HST service that ran between St Pancras and Sheffield in 1988.

Below: Deep in the county from which its train takes its name is No. 7804 *Baydon Manor* at Narberth in September 1963.
COLOUR-RAIL

(THE) PINES EXPRESS

One of England's best-loved trains

A MUCH-lamented train from a much lamented line – that was the 'Pines Express', whose name will forever be synonymous with the Somerset & Dorset line.

The roots of 'The Pines' lay in a joint venture in 1910 between three different railways (one of which was a joint railway in its own right). They were the London & North Western, the Midland Railway and the Somerset & Dorset Joint Railway, which, in October of that year, began working a through restaurant car train from Manchester to Bournemouth.

Grouping in 1923 put the LNWR and MR under the same LMS management and, as the MR had been co-owner of the S&DJ, the LMS now had almost total control of the route and the train.

In 1927, it was decided to give the service a name based on an area of pine trees it passed through in the Bournemouth area and it made its maiden run as a titled train on September 26 that year. In those pre-war days, departure from Manchester London Road was at 10.10am and, at various points along its journey, through coaches were attached or detached, including ones from Liverpool to Southampton and Bradford to Southampton, which were dropped off at Birmingham New Street and Cheltenham respectively.

The S&D section started at Bath and it is that section of severely-graded line through the Mendip hills that so many enthusiasts associate with the 'Pines Express'. By the time the train pulled into Bournemouth West station, it had been on the go for a shade under 6½ hours. The northbound train was scheduled to complete the trip a little faster, in 6¼ hours, despite having to stop at Bromsgrove for a shove up the Lickey incline. Alternative routes in and around Birmingham were sometimes

THE PEAK EXPRESS

THIS London St Pancras to Manchester service began, like 'The Palatine', in 1938, and ran from the capital at 10.30am to Manchester Central via Derby.

In the up direction, the train departed Manchester at 4.25pm and running just ahead of 'The Palatine', which left five minutes later. Both services were suspended at the outbreak of war, but whereas 'The Palatine' was resurrected, 'The Peak Express' disappeared without trace.

(THE) PEMBROKE COAST EXPRESS *

THIS was a service introduced by BR on June 8, 1953 to serve Pembroke Dock. Departure time from Paddington was 10.55am and from Pembroke Dock 7.45am, but within a year of its launch it had been accelerated to cover the 133-mile London-Newport section at well over a mile-a-minute, to become the fastest-ever regular steam-hauled train over that stretch of line. The service experienced more timing changes but existed for more than a decade, losing its name in Western Region timetable re-organisations on September 7, 1963.

The title was resuscitated in 1985 (as the 'Pembroke

Given a cheery wave as it makes its way through Sturminster Newton on September 3, 1962, is the 'Pines Express', headed by unrebuilt 'West Country' Pacific No. 34043 *Combe Martin*. R C RILEY

taken at weekends or whenever required.

In common with the vast majority of titled trains, 'the Pines' was suspended during the war, and although the service reappeared on October 7, 1946, it wasn't until May 23, 1949, that it became a named train once again.

The BR period saw some interesting motive power changes south of Bath, with Southern Region Light Pacifics putting in appearances alongside (and often coupled to) ex-LMS types. BR Standard classes also featured, including 9Fs for the last three summers.

For a period in the 1950s, the northbound 'Pines' terminated in Manchester Mayfield station to ease congestion at London Road. At the other end of the route, the express was routed away from the S&D line in September 1962, finding its way to Bournemouth via Birmingham Snow Hill, Oxford, Reading and Basingstoke. (From October 4, 1965, it terminated in Poole.)

BOURNEMOUTH

Stockport · Macclesfield · Stoke-on-Trent · Stafford · Wolverhampton · Birmingham New Street · Birmingham International · Coventry · Leamington Spa · Banbury · Oxford · Reading · Basingstoke · Winchester · Southampton Airport Parkway · Southampton Central · Brockenhurst · Bournemouth

The Pines Express

Without its principal through train, the S&D line began to struggle and closure came on March 7, 1966. The 'Pines Express' lost its name on March 4, 1967, although the re-routed services steadily expanded and, indeed, even saw a resuscitation of the original title when BR introduced a Manchester-Bournemouth service via Birmingham New Street in 1992. That name survived into the Virgin Trains era, 2002.

Above: A memento of the far more modern Virgin Trains version of 'The Pines Express', itself now consigned to history.

Coast Holiday Express') and, having reverted to its original title, remains in use for a summer Saturday HST service operated by First Great Western, leaving Paddington at 08.45 and Pembroke Dock at 10.00.

'PORTS TO PORTS EXPRESS'

AN unofficial name for an extraordinary cross-country train that began running from Newcastle-upon-Tyne to Barry, Wales, in May 1906.

So called because it connected the docks of Tyneside with those of South Wales, it used tracks owned by several railway companies, including the North Eastern, the Swinton & Knottingley Joint and the Great Central, as far as Woodford. It then meandered in very 'un-express' fashion along a 44-mile single-track Great Western secondary line via Stow-on-the-Wold in order to regain main line metals at Cheltenham. At the end of its journey, it ran over the metals of the Barry Railway.

After a gap caused by the First World War, the train was extended to Swansea (396 miles and 11¼ hrs from Newcastle), via the Vale of Glamorgan line between Barry and Bridgend. Another suspension came for WWII, but

by 1947 the train had disappeared from the LNER timetable.

(PORTSMOUTH EXPRESS)

(*Brand name*): A Class 442 'Wessex Electric' service between London Waterloo and Portsmouth that ran from 1989 and 1992.

THE PRINCIPALITY

THIS train was unusual in that it ran through three different countries – Scotland, England and Wales.

Launched by British Rail's Cross Country sector in the 1980s, it started its journey in two portions, leaving Edinburgh at 12.40 and Glasgow at 12.45, combining usually at Carlisle. It then called at Preston, Crewe, Birmingham, Bristol Parkway and Newport, arriving in the capital of the Principality of Wales at 19.53 (sometimes continuing to Swansea) .

Although it had a northbound equivalent, that train carried a different name ('The Caledonian').

'The Principality' was in service as a titled train from 1984/5 to 1987.

PROVINCIAL EXPRESS

FOR one year – 1990 – the Holyhead-Cardiff service previously known as 'The Welshman' ('Y Cymro') was renamed the 'Provincial Express' and ran that year under the new title but with a silver Welsh dragon logo on its carriage destination labels.

PULLMAN LIMITED EXPRESS

ALTHOUGH cars provided by and operated by the Pullman Car Company had been coupled within the rakes of British trains since 1874, it wasn't until December 5, 1881, that the UK's first *all*-Pullman train was introduced by the London Brighton & South Coast Railway.

This was the 'Pullman Limited Express' (the word Limited referring to the fact that seats needed to be booked in advance and were therefore limited in number).

The title was an official one from the start, having been agreed between LBSCR and Pullman officials in Brighton on November 25 that year, although the Pullman company didn't always use the word 'Express' in its own publicity over the years.

Following an advance press run via Horsham on December 1, the train ran main line from London to Brighton, leaving Victoria every weekday at 10am and 3.50pm and Brighton at 1.20pm and 5.45pm, and was in existence for six years to 1887. On Sundays from February 1882, the same Pullman trainset was attached to ordinary LBSCR first class carriages at Victoria and operated as the 'Pullman Drawing Room Car Train'.

From December that year, ordinary first class carriages were attached to the weekday Pullman train too, although it retained its title.

In 1898, the Sunday service was formally relaunched as the 'Pullman Limited Express' when the 10.45am London to Brighton and Worthing service was divided into two trains, a Pullman one leaving Victoria at 11am and a first class one five minutes later. In the return direction, they left at 9pm and 9.05pm respectively. Christmas Day fell on a Sunday that year and both trains operated.

In November 1908, the weekday 'Pullman Limited

Below: Doing its best to melt the snow at Hullavington, Wiltshire in 1956 is a fiery 'Red Dragon', hauled by 'Britannia' No. 70028 *Royal Star*.
COLOUR-RAIL

(THE) QUEEN OF SCOTS

Attractive names attract the custom

ATTRACTIVE names certainly attract custom, conveying as they do a sense of quality and prestige, and Britain's titled trains have on the whole, been able to boast some fine appellations.

Such was the case with the regally-named 'Queen of Scots', one of the crack Pullman expresses of the East Coast Main Line.

The title was introduced on December 1, 1927, as a re-naming of the 'Harrogate and Edinburgh Pullman' (which had started life in July 1923 as the 'Harrogate Pullman' and been extended to Edinburgh two years later, after which it had unofficially become known as the 'Edinburgh Pullman').

On May 1, 1928, the 'Queen of Scots' was further extended to Glasgow Queen Street. With a departure from London at 11.15am, it was in Glasgow at 8.45pm, having undertaken a marathon journey of just over 450 miles. The up train left Queen Street at 10.05am and was booked to reach the 'Cross at 7.35. In both directions, the Leeds-London run was non-stop.

The locomotives most associated with those relatively short-length Pullman trains (south of Leeds) were the Ivatt C1 class Atlantics, which were used as the heavier Gresley Pacifics were banned from running to Leeds in those days.

Upon the outbreak of war, the 'Queen of Scots' was suspended until July 5, 1948, after which it became a much longer and heavier train, usually handled by new Peppercorn A1 Pacifics south of Leeds, with starting times of 12noon from King's Cross and 10.50am from Glasgow. North of Leeds, motive power was normally an A3, while between Edinburgh and Glasgow, B1s, BR5s and LM5s shared duties with the Pacifics.

Above: Bringing its rake of umber & cream 'Queen of Scots' stock around Wortley south curve in July 1960 is Peppercorn A1 Pacific No. 60123 *H A Ivatt*. GAVIN MORRISON

The definite article was added to the title in BR days and it also carried an elaborate tailboard supplied by the Pullman company itself.

With patronage in the North and Scotland starting to fall off in the 1960s due to relatively slow journey times, BR decided to cut the service back to Harrogate. As Scotland was no longer part of the itinerary, the title had to be dropped and the service was renamed 'The White Rose' – which had hitherto been carried by another train.

The last 'Queen of Scots' ran on June 13, 1964, although in recent years, the name has been used in Scotland for a private luxury 'land cruise' train aimed primarily at American tourists.

The older LNER version of the headboard seen on Gresley Pacific No. 2555 *Centenary* at Leeds Central in June 1938. COLOUR-RAIL Top right: The train's 1920s poster

Express' became the 'Southern Belle', but for some years before introduction of that train, the LBSC informally referred to the Sunday working as the 'Pullman Limited' or the 'Brighton Limited' – in fact, under the latter title, it was described by *The Railway Magazine* in 1903 as one of the "world's most famous trains".

THE RED DRAGON *

CELEBRATING an emblem of Wales, 'The Red Dragon' title was conferred by BR's Western Region upon the 7.30am Carmarthen-Paddington and the 5.55pm return (although in practice the main train started and terminated at Swansea, with only a through portion working west of there to Carmarthen).

The titled service began on June 5, 1950 and was withdrawn 15 years later, on June 12, 1965.

It was resurrected in 1983/4, became 'The Red Dragon Executive' in 1986 and, two years later, 'The Red Dragon Pullman' (although the latter version of the name is not thought to have appeared on carriage destination labels).

Today, the name 'Red Dragon' is still in use – on Great Western's 07.30 Carmarthen-Paddington and 17.15 return.

THE RED ROSE

THE Festival of Britain in 1951 was a chance for Britons to shrug off the memories of the 1940s and look forward to the future. BR certainly entered into the spirit, for a number of named trains made their appearance in connection with those ceremonies.

One was 'The Red Rose', which took its name from the emblem of Lancashire and was doubtless a counter to the East Coast route's 'White Rose', which had given Yorkshire a train related to its own emblem just two years earlier.

The 'Red Rose' name was bestowed upon the 12.05pm Euston-Liverpool express and the 5.25pm return, which for years had been one of the fastest trains on the LMS. The timing of the festival meant that it made its maiden run mid-timetable, on May 3, and special literature was printed bearing the festival logo.

This train was more often than not diagrammed for haulage by 'Princess Royal' class locomotives. Its last run was on April 16, 1966.

■ In 1994/5, BR InterCity produced a set of window labels carrying the title 'The Red Rose Pullman'. They were intended for a Euston-Carlisle service (first stop Warrington), but although two designs were printed, it is not thought they were ever used.

61 PADDINGTON
THE REGATTA EXPRESS

Manchester Piccadilly
Ipswich—Stowmarket—Bury St. Edmunds—Ely—
March—Peterborough—Grantham—Nottingham—
Alfreton & Mansfield Parkway—Chesterfield—
Sheffield—Stockport

The Rhinelander

Above: The modern electronic and digital era has produced the technology to enable train operators to name trains without having to worry about headboards or adhesive window labels, yet few have taken the opportunity. In the 1990s, Thames Trains honoured one of its Henley-Paddington-services with the name 'The Regatta Express'. The main picture shows the apparently anonymous 'Thames Turbo' and the close-up in the inset shows the destination display.
Pictures: HUGH BALLANTYNE and DAVID HULL

THE REGATTA EXPRESS

THE last two or three decades have seen the demise not only of headboards and roofboards, but even the majority of carriage destination window labels, which have been made redundant by the presence on many modern trains of digital electronic panels on the front and/or sides of rolling stock. 'The Regatta Express' was an early example of a train title appearing on the front of modern DMUs, in this case Class 166 'Thames Turbos'.

Taking its name from the annual regatta that takes place at Henley-on-Thames, it ran as the 07.33 from Henley to London Paddington between 1993 and 1996 and was operated by BR Western Region just prior to the takeover of Paddington suburban services by the Thames Trains franchisee.

THE REGENCY BELLE

A PULLMAN train that ran between London Victoria and Brighton for four weeks in March/April 1964. It was unusual in that it operated some days with 5-BEL EMU stock and other days with steam traction and loco-hauled carriages. The train ran only seven times, leaving Victoria at 7.15pm and returning in the early hours of the following morning.

THE RHINELANDER

ONE of several names used by Harwich to Manchester boat train services. This one succeeded 'The European' and started in May 1987, but lasted only 12 months before giving way to 'The Loreley'. Its departure times were 07.20 Harwich-Manchester Piccadilly and 15.27 return.

In the 1980s, the train was routed via Stowmarket, Peterborough, Grantham, Alfreton, Sheffield and Stockport and was usually hauled by a Class 47.

'THE RIO'

AT the height of the West Coast Main Line upgrade in the early part of the 21st century, travel between Manchester and London Euston was often disrupted. So the Strategic Rail Authority and the Midland Mainline TOC co-operated to provide direct Manchester-London services to London St Pancras via the Hope Valley line. Formed of Midland Mainline HSTs, these trains became known semi-officially as "Rios", taking their name from England footballer Rio Ferdinand, who in 2002 had also moved across the Pennines by transferring from Leeds United to Manchester United.

THE BEST YEAR

ALTHOUGH the 1950s was the golden decade for titled trains, the best single year was 1927.

In those 12 months, the 'Big Four' companies launched between them no fewer than 22 named services. The red letter day was undoubtedly July 11, which witnessed the official birth of both 'The Royal Scot' and the 'Flying Scotsman'.

Although some of the trains were all-new, most of the titles were bestowed upon services that had been running in anonymity for many years and which the companies felt merited public recognition.

Right: Bearing one of the least photographed of all headboards – that of the 'The Regency Belle' – is 'Battle of Britain' Pacific No. 34088 *213 Squadron*, pictured at Nine Elms shed on April 11, 1961. This train was in operation for only four weeks, running mostly at night. RODNEY LISSENDEN

Nicely framed within the overall roof of St Pancras station on September 26, 1961 is 'Peak' diesel-electric No. D100 *Sherwood Forester*, having arrived with 'The Robin Hood' from Nottingham. NRM.

THE ROBIN HOOD *

FOR such a large city, Nottingham does not feature too many times in this survey, although it was served by the 'Thames-Forth Express' and, in BR days, by 'The Waverley'. In the late 1950s, however, it did receive a titled train of its own – although, like 'The Nottingham Executive' 30 years later, it was to be a relatively short-lived one.

This was 'The Robin Hood', named after the city's most famous historical character.

A version of the train, originating in Sheffield, had actually been in the timetable since the Midland Railway era and its non-stop run from Nottingham to St Pancras had made it popular with Midlands businessmen, but it wasn't until February 2, 1959, that the train began to start from Nottingham. This decision was made easier for the Midland Region by the fact that 'The Master Cutler' had by then been diverted to run to London via the Eastern Region.

'The Robin Hood' left the city's Midland station each morning at 8.15am and picked up at the village station of Manton, returning from the capital at 4.45pm. Within a few months, 'Peak' Type 4 diesels took over, but it nevertheless proved to be a very short-lived named train, losing its title on September 7, 1962.

The service was revived by BR in 1990 (albeit known for part of that year as the 'Nottingham Pullman'). Other names it carried at various times over the next decade or so included 'The Robin Hood Pullman'. It ran as far as Sheffield, Wakefield and Leeds.

In the Privatisation era, East Midlands Trains has relaunched 'The Robin Hood' and its current departure times are 07.50 from Nottingham and 16.15 from St Pancras.

NAMED FREIGHT TRAINS

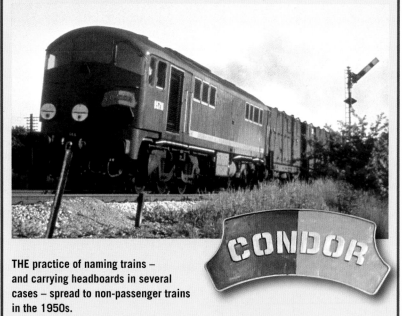

THE practice of naming trains – and carrying headboards in several cases – spread to non-passenger trains in the 1950s.

The most famous by far was 'The Condor', whose name was derived from CONtainers DOoR to door. It was launched in March 1959 and ran from Hendon (London) to Glasgow Gushetfaulds, often hauled by Metropolitan-Vickers Type 2 Co-Bo locomotives.

Other titled freight trains included:
- The Birmingham Braked
- The Blue Spot
- Blue Star Fish Special
- The Bristol
- Chiltern Night Trader
- East Essex Enterprise
- Euro Scot
- Fenland Freighter
- The Fifer
- Galloway Piper
- The Geordie
- Green Arrow
- Heilan Piper
- The Humber-Clyde
- The Killie
- The King's Cross Freighter

- The Kitty
- The Lea Valley Enterprise
- Lothian Piper
- Night Trader
- Tartan Arrow
- Tees-Thames Freighter
- Tees-Tyne Freighter
- Tyne-Tees Freighter
- The "Sweep" (nickname)
- The "Windcutter" (nickname)

Brand names in the world of non-passenger trains included Speedfreight, Speedlink, Red Star, Enterprise and Freightliner (the latter still in operation as a private company).

There were also several semi-officially named postal trains, including: The Capitals Mail (King's Cross-Edinburgh) and the West Coast Postal, which in LMS days (and from 1952 to 1967) sometimes had a four-coach passenger section attached. It is therefore also mentioned in the main directory.

Top of page: 'The Condor' was often placed into the trust of one of the temperamental Metro-Vick Co-Bos. COLOUR-RAIL

Left: 'The King's Cross Freighter' headboard is carefully adjusted by a crew member at Newcastle before the train sets off for the capital.

A lovely summer setting in south Devon as 'Castle' 4-6-0 No. 5049 *Earl of Plymouth* climbs Dainton bank with the westbound 'Royal Duchy' on July 1, 1957. R C RILEY

LMS "ROYAL HIGHLANDER" APPROACHES ABERDEEN
BY
NORMAN WILKINSON, R.I.

THE ROYAL HIGHLANDER

THE famous 'Race to Aberdeen' of 1895 had been won by the West Coast companies with a train that had left Euston at 8pm and arrived in Aberdeen at 4.32 the next morning. Although it had been reduced to just three coaches, it is generally thought of as the service that eventually became 'The Royal Highlander'.

The 'Royal Highlander' sleeping car train formally received its title on September 26, 1927, by which time it had grown into a much longer and slower train. Leaving Euston in the middle of the evening (times varied with the seasons), this LMS leviathan was so well patronised that, in summer, not one but two relief trains had to be run. The main train ran to Inverness, but called at Perth to detach coaches for Aberdeen.

During the 1939-45 period, the train and its relief workings became indispensible for conveying troops and supplies for the war effort, although the main train lost its official name during the hostilities. It wasn't restored until June 17, 1957.

Officially, the train made its last titled run on May 12, 1985, but marketing and publicity material continued to keep the brand alive as a sleeping car service until 1996. Today, its natural descendant, the 'Caledonian Sleeper', still leaves Euston for Inverness every night.

Changing times: By 1959, 'The Royal Duchy' was in the care of diesel-hydraulics such as No. D604 *Cossack*. RM ARCHIVE

A train whose naming required the consent of the Queen

ONE of the trains created in the Western Region's spate of train namings between 1955 and 1957 was possibly unique in requiring the consent of Her Majesty the Queen before it could be authorised.

This was because the WR wished to incorporate the arms of the Duchy of Cornwall on the headboard. Permission was duly granted and 'The Royal Duchy' took to the rails on January 28, 1957. The service on which the title had been conferred was the 11am Penzance-London and 1.30pm return.

The named BR express ceased to run in 1965 but was revived in 1987. Today, an HST of that name is run Mondays to Fridays by First Great Western as the 12.06 Paddington-Penzance and 14.00 ex-Penzance.

An unusual shot of a loco bearing two headboards from the same train at the same time: Thanks to an opportunistic photographer, No. 46235 *City of Birmingham* was adorned with matching 'Royal Highlander' plates at Crewe North shed in 1958. COLOUR-RAIL

PULLMANS THAT WEREN'T

IN May 1985, British Rail (which had bought the rights to the Pullman title in January 1963) relaunched the name as an upmarket brand for its InterCity business trains.

Most of the luxurious heavyweight Pullman cars of old had been withdrawn by then, so the new train titles were somewhat misleading, although InterCity's first-class service did offer at-seat meals.

However, the need to maximise rolling stock utilisation on a busy rail system meant that some trains advertised as Pullmans ended up being formed of standard trainsets, while passengers on ordinary trains ofen found themselves sitting unexpectedly in "posh" carriages.

■ PULLMAN CAR NAMES: Over the years, the Pullman cars themselves have borne some lovely individual names in their own right: In the BR era alone, these have included: Alicante, Amber, Amethyst, Belinda, Cassandra, Clementina, Cygnus, Cynthia, Eagle, Emerald, Falcon, Fortuna, Glencoe, Hawk, Hercules, Hibernia, Ibis, Iolanthe, Isle of Thanet, Juno, Maid of Kent, Malaga, Medusa, Minerva, Octavia, Onyx, Opal, Pearl, Pegasus, Penelope, Perseus, Phoenix, Rainbow, Robin, Ruby, Sapphire, Sunbeam, Swift, Topaz, Zena, Zenobia, Diamond Bar, Pegasus Bar and Hadrian Bar.

The most famous train on the West Coast route

Two for the price of one: 'Royal Scot' class loco No. 46140 *The King's Royal Rifle Corps'* gets under way after taking over the up 'Royal Scot' express from 'Princess Coronation' No. 46222 *Queen Mary* outside Carlisle Kingmoor sheds circa 1956. The Pacific has one of the elaborate 'tartan' versions of 'Royal Scot' headboard.
RAIL PHOTOPRINTS

ASK the proverbial 'man or woman in the street' to name a titled train and the chances are that many would have a stab at the 'Flying Scot' or the 'Royal Scot'. The first, of course, never existed, except in a surprisingly large number of mistaken memories, but the other name represented one of the most successful brand names ever marketed.

This West Coast rival to the 'Flying Scotsman' could trace its history back to the 1860s too, although, surprisingly, the name wasn't officially conferred on the train until July 11, 1927 – the year the LMS's eponymous 'Royal Scot' locomotives began to appear on the scene. Like its famous East Coast competitor, the train had a time-honoured London departure of 10am for many years.

It was as rivalry between the LMS and the LNER heated up in the late 1920s and early '30s that the 'Royal Scot' really began to hit the headlines and, on April 27, 1928, as a publicity stunt, its Glasgow and Edinburgh portions were divided in London, instead of at the remote Scottish junction of Symington, and run separately – both being hauled non-stop for distances of 401 and 399 miles respectively!

Those extraordinary feats were performed to try to steal the thunder of the LNER and its new corridor tender-fitted Pacifics and couldn't possibly have been sustained on a regular basis, of course, but, in 1932, the 1895 agreement restricting the West and East Coast companies to an 8¼-hour minimum Anglo-Scottish time came to an end, and, in the years that followed, the 'Royal Scot', along with other famous LMS expresses, began to be accelerated to more realistic and competitive speeds.

Headlines were made again in 1933 when a 'Royal Scot' coaching set and locomotive were sent across the Atlantic for an 11,000-mile publicity tour of the USA.Following the war, the train's title was formally restored by BR on February 16, 1948, and, later that year, the express began to reflect changing times when it was hauled on a number of occasions by the two new diesel-electric locomotives, Nos. 10000 and 10001.

By 1960, dieselisation and load restrictions had allowed the down train to be speeded up by 40 minutes and the Euston departure time was

In the 1950s, 'The Royal Scot' could sometimes be seen in the care of 'the twins' – LMS-designed diesel-electric sisters 10000 and 10001, here waiting to leave a rainy Euston in 1958. COLOUR-RAIL

Above: A special train requires a special setting and Glasgow Central station had its own 'Royal Scot gate'.

Right: This rare headboard was introduced when double-headed 'D400s' began working the train on May 4, 1970. It was used for only the first week of the accelerated service. ALLAN C BAKER

accordingly changed to 9.05am, later altered to 10.05. By 1968, by which time the train was benefiting from electric haulage on the southern end of the WCML, new Class 50 diesels began hauling the Crewe-Glasgow section, later double-heading in order to maintain improved schedules.

In the mid-1970s, the 'Royal Scot' was lumped in by the BR marketing department as one of several 'Electric Scots', but retained its name right up into the Privatisation and Virgin Trains era and didn't finally lose it until June 1, 2002.

For a while between 1982 and 1998, the up service sometimes contained a portion from Ayr.

■ For one season only – winter 1987-88 – the train's title was modified to 'The Royal Scot Limited'.

By way of a change, this shot shows a British titled train in America – and the different style of headboard adopted especially for that ambassadorial tour in 1933. The loco purporting to be No. 6100 *Royal Scot* was in fact No. 6152 *The King's Dragoon Guardsman*. *RM* ARCHIVE

Right: Overtaking a suburban EMU near Clapham Junction in the 1950s is 'West Country' No. 34095 *Brentor*, sporting the large Southern Region-style headboard of 'The Royal Wessex'.

THE ROYAL WESSEX

WHEN peace returned to Britain after the war, the Southern Railway elected not to reinstate the non-stop 'Bournemouth Limited', but to launch a new express on the same route, starting from Weymouth at 7.38am and calling at Bournemouth, Southampton and Winchester.

Inaugurated on October 1, 1945, it ran anonymously until May 3, 1951, when, in conjunction with that year's Festival of Britain, it was christened 'The Royal Wessex'.

In 1957, a two-hour schedule more in keeping with that of the pre-war 'Bournemouth Limited' was introduced and, by 1960, the 'Royal Wessex' had become the heaviest regular working on the Bournemouth line, with its 13 coaches (including through portions for Swanage and Weymouth) normally requiring a Class 8 'Merchant Navy' Pacific. But the standardisation that came with electrification of the route meant that it couldn't continue and its final run as a titled train was made on July 8, 1967.

However, in May 1988, when the line from Bournemouth to Weymouth was electrified and the Class 442 'Wessex Electrics' were introduced, the name was resurrected by Network SouthEast to draw attention to the fact that Weymouth had become realistically commutable for the first time. It left the Dorset coast at 06.03 and returned from Waterloo at 17.15. In both directions, a stop was made at Southampton Central to attach/detach a Poole stopping portion.

THE SAINT DAVID *

NAMED after the patron saint of Wales, this train was originally inaugurated in May 1984 as a BR InterCity 125 service between Paddington and Swansea.

The suffix 'Executive' was added in 1986 but changed to 'Pullman' from October '88 to October '89 (although the latter version was never printed on carriage labels and is thought to have been a confusion brought about by InterCity's use of the Pullman brand logo). Another variant in InterCity days was 'St David Shuttle'.

Today, the train (officially minus the 'Pullman' part of the title) is still operated as First Great Western's 07.45 Paddington-Swansea and 11.28 return.

It should be noted that over the years, the spelling of 'Saint' has fluctuated between that and the abbreviated 'St', especially where window labels are concerned.

THE SAINT MUNGO

THIS train was one of two new weekday expresses introduced by the LMS on July 5, 1937 to cover the 153-mile Glasgow-Aberdeen run in just three hours (the other was 'The Bon Accord'). Departing from Aberdeen at 9.35am and Glasgow at 1.30pm, it was usually hauled by one of the then-new 'Jubilee' 4-6-0s and was limited to eight coaches, including a restaurant car, weighing 260 tons tare in order to maintain the demanding schedule over difficult terrain.

The train's name – which commemorated the patron saint of Glasgow – was dropped on the outbreak of war in September 1939 but resurrected by British Railways on May 23, 1949 – albeit for a different service, the 9.35am from Aberdeen and 5pm ex-Buchanan Street.

From June 1962, the title was used to describe the 5.30pm Glasgow-Aberdeen and the 9.30am in the opposite direction. Upon closure of Buchanan Street on November 7, 1966, the service ran to Glasgow Queen Street.

Its last run as a titled train took place on May 4, 1968, eight months to the day after closure to passenger services of the Caledonian main line between Stanley Junction and Kinnaber Junction, although by then the headboards had long ceased to be carried by the locomotives.

Below: In addition to its London Midland Region duties (see page 84), LMS-design No. 10000 also spent time on the Southern Region and among the trains it worked was 'The Royal Wessex', pictured in 1954. COLOUR-RAIL

(THE) SCANDINAVIAN

THIS LNER boat train started life as the 'Esbjerg Continental Express' on September 24, 1928, became the 'Scandinavian Continental Express' two years later and had its name shortened to this final version in May 1931.

It connected London Liverpool Street with Harwich Parkeston Quay, where passengers transferred to ferries for the Danish port of Esbjerg.

When the train first started, it was a summer service only. In winter, passengers were conveyed in a portion of the 3.10pm London-Yarmouth, which was detached at Manningtree and worked to Harwich by another loco, but eventually the train became an all-round service. It was primarily an afternoon working, with London departures varying between 3 and 4pm and up departures approximating to lunchtime, depending on the season.

In common with all other European boat trains, it was withdrawn once war broke out in September 1939, but was resumed at an early opportunity, on December 7, 1945, and continued for 30 years, right through into the modern traction era, until May 4, 1975.

'The Scandinavian' is notable for having carried at least seven variants of headboard design during its pre-and post-war existence.

SCANDINAVIAN CONTINENTAL EXPRESS

THE name by which 'The Scandinavian' was known in 1931 (see previous entry).

(THE) SCARBOROUGH FLYER (FLIER)

IN an attempt to bring the seaside attractions of Scarborough to the citizens of London, the LNER introduced in 1923 an 11.50am restaurant car express from King's Cross that would travel non-stop as far as York and get them to the Yorkshire resort at 4.20pm, in good time to settle into hotels and boarding houses.

The return leg of this summer-only train was timed equally conveniently at 3pm (thus allowing an extra

Above: With Harwich docks in the background, B12 4-6-0 No. 61533 sets off for London Liverpool Street with 'The Scandinavian' in the mid-1950s. Painting by MALCOLM ROOT

Above and below: A train whose name was spelt two ways: The LNER's 'Scarborough Flier' runs over Langley troughs behind Gresley Pacific No. 4480 *Enterprise* in the early 1930s, while (below), BR's 'Scarborough Flyer' emerges from Stoke tunnel behind classmate No. 60047 *Donovan* in July 1959. RAIL ARCHIVE STEPHENSON and COLOUR-RAIL

morning of bathing if desired) with arrival back in the capital at 7.30.

The train was one of the fastest on the LNER and the company decided after four years to boost its public profile by officially naming it. The christening was, however, marred by split identity, for the LNER seemed unsure of the correct spelling, using the term 'Scarborough Flier' on the loco headboards and 'Scarborough Flyer' in timetables and on publicity material.

The first run as a titled train took place on July 11, 1927, and, over the next decade, the train – which was almost invariably Pacific-hauled on the East Coast Main Line section – flew ever faster until the London-York leg had been brought down to just three hours, giving a total time of 3hr 55min to Scarborough Central or 4hr 50min by through coach to Whitby Town.

In 1937, the LNER approved the building of two dedicated trainsets and, by 1939, two Scarborough-bound expresses were leaving King's Cross, one at 10.50 and another 10 minutes later. War soon intervened, however, and the title was suspended, not being reinstated until June 5, 1950, when BR took the opportunity not only to harmonise the spelling on the 'y' form but to add the definite article.

The 'Flyer' petered out as a named train in 1962/63, but a direct service from London continued into the 1980s – and, of course, the main line preserved steam era of the late 20th and early 21st centuries has seen summer-only 'Scarborough Spa Express' steam specials.

SCARBORO' AND WHITBY EXPRESS

THE predecessor of the 'Scarborough Flier' was referred to by this name in the Great Northern Railway timetable of August 1880. Departure times were 10.30am from King's Cross and 9.15am from Whitby.

"THE SCOTCH EXPRESS"

ANYONE looking back through Victorian and Edwardian newspapers will gain the impression that virtually every Anglo-Scottish passenger train was called 'The Scotch Express', regardless of which route it ran on!

Insofar as it appeared frequently in the pages of Bradshaw's timetables, it is indeed a train title – but not one in the accepted sense, as it applied not to a single service but to numerous trains. It was, for example, the 'Scotch Express' that was wrecked on the West Coast at Preston in 1896 and the 'Scotch Express' that was wrecked on the East Coast at Grantham 10 years later! There was even said to be a train of that name plying between Plymouth and Aberdeen.

In truth, it was mainly a nickname coined by the 19th century popular press and doesn't appear to have enjoyed full official status with any railway company, although it did occasionally appear in the small print of some company literature and in the columns of Victorian and Edwardian timetables. The phrase is particularly common on contemporary postcards and artwork (the Midland Railway's 'Morning Scotch Express' for example). Even the 'Royal Scot' was sometimes referred to as the 'Scotch Express'.

See also 'Special Scotch Express'

'THE SCOTSMAN'

A SERVICE of this name is understood to have run for a brief time from London St Pancras to Glasgow.

THE SCOTTISH PULLMAN

INTRODUCED by British Rail from September 30, 1991, this name was applied to two different services – the 08.00 King's Cross-Glasgow Central and 14.00 return, and also the 06.00 Edinburgh Waverley-King's Cross and 15.00 return (the times varied over the years). The title was discontinued in 2004.

THE SEVERN-TYNE

A SHORT-lived service, inaugurated by BR in 1970, which left Weston-super-Mare at 07.20 and returned from Newcastle at 16.20. From May 1971, it was extended at both ends of its journey to run from Paignton to Edinburgh and was duly renamed the 'Torbay-Forth'.

AMBULANCE TRAIN

THERE was a named ambulance train on the LNER towards the end of the Second World War, which bore the name 'The Knight Errant'.

THE SHAKESPEARE EXPRESS

THIS was a Great Western Railway service that ran between the wars and linked Stratford-upon-Avon direct with London Paddington. Not to be confused with the 'William Shakespeare'.

A summer-only service, it had only a short existence, lasting from 1928 to 1931.

THE SHAMROCK

THE shamrock, a traditional emblem of Ireland, lent its name in 1954 to the 8.10am Liverpool Lime Street to Euston and the 4.55pm return.

On weekdays, the down train was a non-stop that completed the journey to the Merseyside city in just under three and a half hours, enabling passengers to make connection with the Belfast and Dublin steamers. The train's last run as a titled service was on April 16, 1966.

THE SHEFFIELD CONTINENTAL *

ONE of the few titled trains in operation in 2012, 'The Sheffield Continental' is even rarer among such workings in that its name is a recently-coined one and not a revival of a steam era service. It was chosen as a result of a public competition staged by East Midlands Trains.

Inaugurated in 2008 and formed of an EMT Class 222 'Meridian' DEMU, it leaves 'the steel city' at 06.47, but only the southbound service runs as a titled train.

THE SHEFFIELD PULLMAN

A FIVE-car Pullman train launched by the LNER on June 2, 1924, to run from London to Sheffield via an unusual route – King's Cross-Grantham-Nottingham Victoria and thence to Sheffield Victoria by the ex-GC main line.

Departure from the capital was at 11.05am and the steel city was reached at 2.20pm with the return leaving at 4.45pm for an 8pm arrival.

After just a month, the diagram was reversed so that the train left Sheffield in the morning and returned in the evening. The following year, Nottingham was removed from the itinerary and the train became instead the 'Sheffield and Manchester Pullman' (better known as the 'Manchester Pullman'), running via Retford.

That service was withdrawn after just five months, in September 1925, and the Pullman rolling stock used to create a new service from King's Cross to Leeds and Bradford (see 'West Riding Pullman').

A third of a century later, in September 1958, the 'Sheffield Pullman' title came back into use when British Railways switched the 'Master Cutler' from the ex-Great Central route to the ex-Great Northern route. To utilise the stock of that train between the peak hours, a midday working from King's Cross to Sheffield was introduced and the brake-end fascia nameboards carried the legend 'Sheffield Pullman', rather than 'Master Cutler'. Two years later, the train was re-equipped with new Metro-Cammell loco-hauled Pullman stock and, in October 1965, it was (along with the 'Cutler'), diverted to use Sheffield Midland.

The 'Sheffield Pullman' was withdrawn for the second time on October 4, 1968.

'THE SHEFFIELD SPECIAL'

AN unofficial name for a Great Central Railway express from Marylebone to Sheffield Victoria and Manchester Central, first run in 1903. The train included slip-coach portions for Grimsby (dropped off at Leicester) and Bradford (slipped at Penistone). The 'Special' continued to run into LNER days but was discontinued in 1939.

Below: A rare shot of 'The Snowdonian' at Bangor on July 14, 1958, showing the train's name on the carriage roofboard. The loco is Stanier 4MT 2-6-4T No. 42627. PATRICK RAWLINSON

THE SNOWDONIAN

A SUMMER-only local service linking Rhyl, Llandudno and Bangor with Llanberis, operational between the mid 1950s and 1962. The carriages carried named roofboards and were sometimes sighted in places such as Crewe and Kidsgrove on summer Saturdays, suggesting that the stock was occasionally used to convey North Staffordshire day-trippers in the morning before spending the middle part of the day shuttling along the North Wales coast.

After a gap of almost a quarter of a century, the title was re-used in the modern traction era for a London Euston-Pwllheli summer service between 1986/7 and 1990.

■ It is understood that another named train, 'The Snowdon Express', ran for a time between Llandudno and Llanberis before the latter station's closure in 1962.

THE SILVER JUBILEE

This train was truly fit for a King

IT is interesting to note that some of the most famous named trains of all – the pre-war streamliners of the LNER and LMS – never carried headboards.

'The Silver Jubilee' was the first of such super-expresses to appear, on September 30, 1935, and made history as the first fully-streamlined train and locomotive combination to run in Great Britain.

Named to mark the 25th anniversary of the reign of King George V, it featured silver-grey livery throughout and ran between King's Cross and Newcastle, leaving the latter city at 10am and the capital at 5.30pm.

Nicknamed "The Silver Bullet" by its passengers, its schedule was four hours each way, inclusive of a stop at Darlington in each direction.

Rarely, if ever, has a new British train captured the public imagination in the way this one did. In fact, so popular was it that the LNER recouped the cost of building it in just two years… from the sale of supplementary fare tickets alone! In 1938, an extra 3rd class coach was inserted to make it an eight-coach train.

The train seemed to reflect the spirit of the times, heralding an optimistic new future after the years of the Depression – a future that was to be cruelly cut short just four years later by the outbreak of war.

Before then, though, Sir Nigel Gresley's masterpiece managed to revolutionise train travel and trigger the rivalry with the London Midland & Scottish Railway that, in 1938, would result in a new world speed record for steam traction. The 'Silver Jubilee's locos and articulated coaching sets were almost incredibly reliable, clocking up well over half a million miles with no serious mishaps and only the occasional engine failure.

A few days before war broke out, the train was withdrawn from the timetables and never returned in that form (although some of its coaches were used in the post-war 'Fife Coast Express').

However, to celebrate the silver jubilee of Queen Elizabeth II in 1977, the title was revived for a year by British Rail and bestowed upon the 7.45am King's Cross-Edinburgh and 3pm return, whose diesel locomotives carried an impressive ceremonial headboard from June 8, 1977 to May 5, 1978.

Right: Even the luggage labels of the 'Silver Jubilee' were classy items.

The pioneer A4, No. 2509 *Silver Link*, at full chat with the 'Silver Jubilee' in the 1930s. What a magnificent spectacle!
Painting by MALCOLM ROOT, who reveals that the location is "a fictitious one that could be anywhere on the GN Main Line".

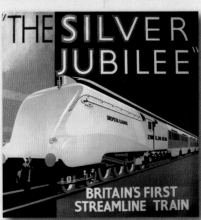

Above: An LNER poster advertising Britain's first streamline train.

Left: To commemorate the Queen's Silver Jubilee in 1977, BR brought the train of that name back for a year and devised a ceremonial headboard especially for fitting to Class 55s, one of which is pictured on the express at Doncaster.
GAVIN MORRISON

Silver Link and the Gresley 'Hush-Hush' 4-6-4 on the High Level Bridge at Newcastle. For just a few weeks in 1935, it would have been theoretically possible for these two innovative locomotive designs to have rubbed shoulders. **Painting by JOHN AUSTIN**

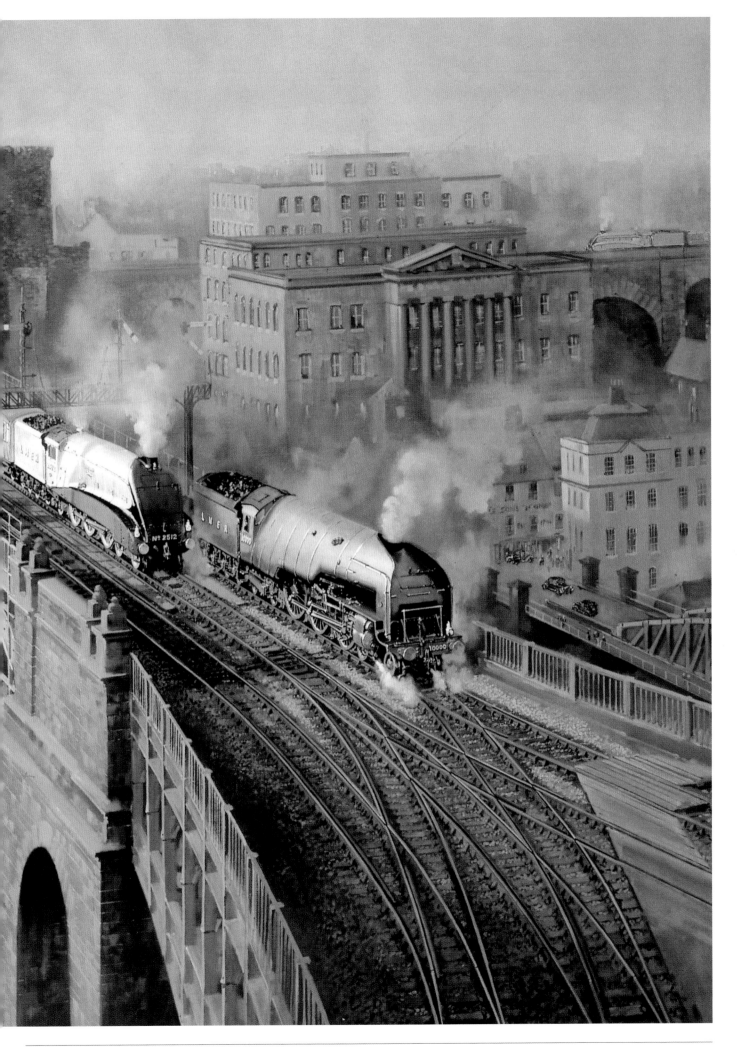

Above: A3 No. 60082 *Neil Gow* nears the summit of Ais Gill with the up 'Thames-Clyde Express'. Painting by CHRIS HOLLAND

Right: After the Second World War, the LNER decided not to reintroduce the famous streamliner 'The Silver Jubilee' – but it did decide to use some of the luxurious silver carriages in very changed circumstances away from the glare of the London media. Five of the coaches (minus valances) are captured by the camera in this rare picture of the 'Fife Coast Express' climbing Cowlairs incline with B1 No. 61402 at the front and a banker in the rear.

Below: Short-lived North British diesel-hydraulic Type 2s stand in the sidings at Newton Abbot as 'Castle' No. 5046 *Earl Cawdor* passes with 'The Torbay Express'. R C RILEY

THE SOUTH EXPRESS

THE Midland & South Western Junction Railway had two named trains – 'The South Express' and 'The North Express'. The was basically a 'mirror-image' of its southbound partner, which, in the half-decade prior to the First World War, ran from Cheltenham Lansdown to Southampton West via Andover Junction. Departure time in the 1913/14 timetable was 1.10pm.

Although its northbound cousin lost its name after the conflict, 'The South Express' continued and in its final year (1922) was running as the 1.35pm Cheltenham Queens Road to Southampton Town.

THE SOUTH COAST EXPRESS

A HASTINGS to Portsmouth Harbour service inaugurated by the London, Brighton & South Coast Railway in 1912.

THE SOUTH WALES EXECUTIVE

AN InterCity 125-formed service run by British Rail InterCity, and later the Great Western TOC, between London Paddington and Swansea in the mid to late-1990s.

THE SOUTH WALES PULLMAN

ALTHOUGH the Great Western Railway had not been a

particularly keen advocate of Pullman trains, its Western Region successors did much to redress the balance under BR custodianship.

'The South Wales Pullman' was launched in the summer of 1955 as an eight-coach set entrusted to the regular care of a 'Castle' class 4-6-0 and linked Swansea, Port Talbot, Cardiff and Newport with London, running non-stop through England.

At first, there was just one return working, leaving Paddington at 9.55am, but, after two years, departure time was changed to 8.50am to enhance the appeal to business travellers.

After six years as a largely steam-hauled service, the train underwent a complete transformation in September 1961 when one of the WR's 'Blue Pullman' diesel units was transferred to the route. In addition to the change of traction, that meant a total reversal of operating procedure, for the morning departure from London was replaced by a 6.40am start from Swansea to capitalise on business demand. Patronage began to grow and in the mid-1960s the service was expanded to three trains a day in each direction.

Numerous timetable recasts, additional station calls and speed improvements followed over the next half-decade, during which time the units lost their blue & white livery in exchange for a rather drab grey & blue. The end came with the demise of the Pullman units in 1973.

Between 1967 and 1973, the service was sometimes referred to informally as the "Swansea Pullman".

SOUTH YORKSHIRE EXECUTIVE

THIS London St Pancras to Sheffield service was introduced by BR's London Midland Region in 1982. Normally HST-formed, it ran until 1989.

THE SOUTH YORKSHIREMAN *

ONE of only two officially-titled trains to operate over the Great Central main line in steam days (the other was the 'Master Cutler'), 'The South Yorkshireman' linked London Marylebone with Halifax and Bradford and so, despite calling at Sheffield en route, could more accurately have

Below: Well-dressed passengers leave the comfort of 'The South Wales Pullman' at Swansea High Street for the last time after arrival of the final down service at the town's High Street station on September 8, 1961. The loco for the historic occasion was 'Castle' 4-6-0 No. 5048 *Earl of Devon*. HUGH BALLANTYNE

Left: Away from the usual glamorous image of titled trains … Low Moor shed's B1 No. 61383 adds to the Yorkshire grime as it slogs up the 1-in-50 between Bradford Exchange and Bowling Junction with 'The South Yorkshireman' on August 15, 1959. GAVIN MORRISON

Setting sail with the 'Northern Belle' land cruise from King's Cross on June 18, 1937, is A4 No. 4489 *Dominion of Canada*. E R WETHERSETT

LAND CRUISES

LAND cruise trains differ from holiday excursions insofar as they do not run for the purpose of taking passengers from A to B via the shortest route and quickest time but instead follow a leisurely meandering course, usually through pleasant scenery and almost invariably over more than one day, with their patrons either spending the night on the train or in nearby hotels. This makes the trains different from railtours, which normally tend to be out and back in a day. Premium fares normally apply.

This is a concept that continues to this day with privately-owned luxury trains, particularly in Scotland, but in the days of the Big Four, the main one was the 'Northern Belle', a headboarded train that ran from

King's Cross to various destinations at weekends between 1929 and 1939.

The following, featuring trains past (and present *), is a selection only. (NB. Some of these tours have taken the titles of historic trains listed in the main directory):

- BRITISH PULLMAN *
- CAMBRIAN RADIO CRUISE
- CLWYD RANGER
- CTAC SCOTTISH TOURS EXPRESS +
- C&O HOTEL EXPRESS ++
- THE GREAT BRITAIN *
- THE HIGHLANDER
- THE HIGHLAND PRINCE
- THE HUMBER ROVER
- THE LOCHIEL

- THE MONARCH OF THE GLEN
- THE NEWCASTLE VENTURER
- NORTHERN BELLE (LNER and modern era *)
- NORTH WALES LAND CRUISE
- NORTH WALES RADIO LAND CRUISE
- PENNINE LIMITED
- QUEEN OF SCOTS *
- ROYAL SCOTSMAN *
- THE STATESMAN *
- STOBART PULLMAN
- WELSH CHIEFTAIN
- WEST HIGHLANDER *

+ (CTAC stood for Creative Travel Agents Conference).
++ This train ran from Glasgow in connection with the Callandar & Oban Hotel.

been called 'The West Yorkshireman'. Introduced as the fledgling BR's first new titled train on May 31, 1948, it was basically a replacement for a pre-war service called 'The Yorkshireman'. Departure from Bradford Exchange in 1948 was at 10am with the return north starting out at 4.50pm. An inter-Regional service, it was often hauled between Sheffield and the West Yorkshire towns by a Stanier locomotive and from Sheffield southwards by an ex-LNER engine.

The title was dropped on January 2, 1960 but, in 2008, East Midlands Trains staged a public competition to find a name for a new service it was introducing and *Railway Magazine* reader Stewart Dalton won by suggesting a revival of 'The South Yorkshireman'.

The train was duly resurrected in December 2008 and continues to run. In the 2012 timetable, it leaves Sheffield at 07.41, formed of an HST, and returns from St Pancras as a 'Meridian' DEMU at 17.55. It is only listed as a titled train in EMT's pocket and Internet-based timetables, not in the printed National Rail version.

SOUTHAMPTON EXPRESS

IN the first decade of the 20th century, the Great Western Railway inaugurated a train of this name, running from Paddington to Southampton Docks. To do so, it must have utilised considerable running powers, as the GWR's nearest points of contact would have been Winchester or Basingstoke.

SOUTHERN BELLE

THE success of a Sundays-only Pullman excursion train that ran between 1898 and 1908 (see 'The Brighton Limited') showed the London Brighton & South Coast Railway that there was potential for a regular week-round service. So the Pullman Company ordered a train of seven new 12-wheelers and, in November 1908, 'The Southern Belle' was launched.

Taking the departure time of its Sunday predecessor, the 'Belle' left London Victoria at 11am but the service was soon doubled by the addition of a second daily return trip, leaving London at 3.10pm. Such was the success of the train that the frequency was increased to three round trips a day at weekends.

After the LBSCR had been absorbed into the Southern Railway in 1923, the new company decided to increase the length of the 'Belle' by the addition of third-class Pullman cars. With a gross weight sometimes exceeding 400 tons, this would have been an exacting challenge for the relatively modest locos of the time, but the Grouping had allowed the SR to draft 'King Arthur' 4-6-0s onto the Brighton line. These handled the service well, but electrification was proceeding apace on Southern metals and the SR thus decided to end the steam-hauled 'Southern Belle' and replace it with an all-new train of electric multiple unit Pullmans.

The last steam-hauled 'Southern Belle' ran on December 31, 1932, and the new electric version entered service the next day. The introduction of the 'Bournemouth Belle' in 1931 had, however, created the potential for confusion among SR passengers, so, on June 29, 1934, the 'Southern Belle' was renamed the 'Brighton Belle'.

'SPECIAL SCOTCH EXPRESS'

THIS was the semi-official term used by the East Coast companies for the 10am King's Cross-Edinburgh and simultaneous southbound service from 1862 to 1927, after which the train was officially named the 'Flying Scotsman'. (It was sometimes also known as the 'Scotch Special').

(STANSTED EXPRESS)

(*Brand name*): A generic term coined by British Rail for its regular-interval London Liverpool Street-Stansted Airport shuttle service.

STARLIGHT EXPRESS

A LATE-1950s/early-1960s overnight service between Glasgow and Euston. Offering cheap tickets, it ran at weekends and holidays only. The title was formally dispensed with in 1986.

(STARLIGHT SPECIAL)

(*Brand name*): This was the generic term for a series of overnight trains laid on by BR for holders of heavily-discounted tickets between 1953 and 1962. They ran from London Marylebone to either Glasgow St Enoch or Edinburgh Waverley. The London terminus was later changed to St Pancras.

The departure time from Marylebone was 10.30pm and, although officially non-stop, the trains often made unscheduled halts at rural junctions to allow ordinary timetabled trains (and even fast fitted freights) to run through without delay

STRANRAER BOAT EXPRESS

See 'The Northern Irishman'.

STRATFORD-UPON-AVON PULLMAN

ONE of several modern era trains graced with 'Pullman' titles even though they're not so officially, this one was a through HST service from Paddington to Stratford, active in 1987.

THE STRATHEARN EXPRESS

INAUGURATED in 1911 by the Caledonian Railway, this train ran from Glasgow to St Fillan's and Crieff and took its name from a district of Perthshire.

THE STRATHPEFFER SPA EXPRESS

IN July 1911, the Highland Railway opened a large hotel in the spa town of Strathpeffer and for the next five summers laid on a return train from Inverness named 'The Strathpeffer Spa Express' (sometimes shortened to 'Strathpeffer Express'). On some days, the train ran from Aviemore and on such occasions would run past Inverness station without stopping. The service is understood to have ceased shortly after the outbreak of the First World War.

STIRLING AND BEN LEDI EXPRESS

DATING back to Caledonian Railway days, this train ran between Glasgow Queen Street and Callandar, a town in the former county of Perthshire. Ben Ledi is the name of a small mountain in the area.

THE SUNNY SOUTH EXPRESS / SPECIAL

FEW train titles can have been as evocative as this one. To coin a modern phrase, 'it really did do what it said on the can' (assuming it wasn't raining of course!) It began life in March 1905 as a restaurant car service operated jointly by the LNWR and LBSCR from Manchester to Brighton and Eastbourne. Within 10 years, the idea of running trains that could take people from the dark satanic mills of the North to the sunny sandy beaches of the South had really caught on – cross-country trains were here to stay.

The express, which ran every day in summer, resumed operation after the First World War, leaving Manchester

Above: Although staged for press and publicity purposes (the names purportedly being exchanged at the front of the train were actually carriage roofboards), this photograph marks the occasion on which the Southern Railway changed the name of the 'Southern Belle' to 'Brighton Belle'– on June 29, 1934. GETTY

Above: 'The Talisman' –
named after a novel by Sir
Walter Scott – at Newcastle
Central behind A3 No.
60061 *Pretty Polly* in May
1960. COLOUR-RAIL

London Road in the morning and taking the West London Line for an arrival in Brighton at around 5pm, after which it continued to Bexhill and Hastings. The northbound service had a similar timing but wasn't in Manchester until after 6pm, having detached a Liverpool portion at Crewe.

The train also ran to the Kent coast; On Fridays and Saturdays in its final year, 1939, it ran to Ramsgate, via Herne Bay and Margate, with through coaches (including an ex-LNWR restaurant car) from Liverpool and Manchester, and returned from Ramsgate on Saturdays and Mondays at 10.50am.

The title of the train was unusual insofar as it was officially known as that by the LBSCR (and by Bradshaws' timetable), but not by its partner railway, the LNWR.

A remarkable spin-off was the discovery, during trials in 1909, that an LBSC Class I3 4-4-2 tank loco hauling seven coaches could run the 90 miles from East Croydon to Rugby without taking water despite having a tank capacity of only 2,100 gallons – one of the 'miraculous' results of superheating.

After the Grouping, various permutations were introduced to give cities such as Bradford and Nottingham direct services to the south coast, but the title 'Sunny South Special' (officially named 'Sunny South Express' in 1927) disappeared at the outbreak of war 12 years later.

(THE) SUSSEX SCOT

MAKING its inaugural run as a named train on May 16, 1988, this was BR's Glasgow/Edinburgh to Brighton via Kensington Olympia service. The northbound train – normally formed of a Class 47 and 10 coaches – left Brighton at 13.15 (later 08.45) and, after switching to electric traction en route, divided at Carstairs into Glasgow and Edinburgh portions, reversing the procedure in the opposite direction. The Carstairs split was later done away with and, in 1994, the train was re-routed to travel via Manchester Piccadilly.

At weekends, it was often routed via Guildford with a reversal at Redhill.

The service was perpetuated by Virgin CrossCountry

for the first five years of Privatisation, but the 'Voyager' revolution brought about the train's demise and the last run took place on September 28, 2002.

"SWANSEA PULLMAN"

See 'South Wales Pullman'.

THE TALISMAN

NAMED after the title of a novel by Sir Walter Scott, this was one of the crack expresses of the East Coast Main Line in the 1950s/60s heyday of titled trains. A fast, limited, service, it was launched on September 17, 1956, as the first titled late-afternoon Edinburgh service from King's Cross since the demise of 'The Coronation' in August 1939.

Like that pre-war streamliner, it was Pacific-hauled and departed at 4pm on Mondays to Fridays only, half an hour earlier than the up service left Edinburgh. The trains, initially of eight coaches, were the first entirely maroon-liveried formations on the East Coast and, in a link with its predecessor, the two sets of stock each included an ex-'Coronation' open first articulated twin. Calling only at Newcastle, the journey time was 6 hours 40 minutes.

In June 1957, the schedule was eased by five minutes and a morning service was added, using the same sets. The trains thus became 'The Morning Talisman' and 'The Afternoon Talisman' for a while, although the 4pm regained its original name during the 12 months from September 1957 when 'The Fair Maid' occupied the morning path. From June 1959, however, both services were titled 'The Talisman'. By now, the morning trains were leaving King's Cross at 7.50am and Edinburgh at 8.30am and were also making additional stops.

Accelerated 'Deltic' timings in June 1962 gave the morning trains an earlier arrival at their destinations and the sets, now 11 coaches, returned at 4pm on a new six-hour schedule.

In the summer of 1964, BR's experimental XP64 set in blue & grey livery formed the 8am up and 4pm down 'Talisman' services whilst first class accommodation in the other set was provided by Pullman cars. September 1964

saw the XP64 set replaced by a similar part-Pullman formation, but Pullmans were withdrawn from the trains seven months later. Also from September 1964 (until April 1966), the first up train started from Glasgow at 1am and the down afternoon train terminated there at 11pm.

During the 'Deltic' period, 'The Talisman' name was dropped in May 1968, but was restored – to the afternoon services only, including a recently-introduced Saturday train – in 1973. This coincided with the fastest diesel loco-hauled timings of 5 hours 40 minutes (down) and 5 hours 45 minutes (up).

HSTs replaced 'Deltics' on May 8, 1978, and, during the next few years, both Glasgow and Aberdeen were variously served by 'The Talisman'. In 1983/84, the down train enjoyed its fastest timing to Edinburgh of 4 hours 44 minutes, including three stops, and the up train was later accelerated to 4 hours 47 minutes from the Scottish capital, with four stops.

In May 1987, the title was transferred from the 16.00 ex-King's Cross to the 08.00 and the up service lost its name in May 1990. Class 91-hauled sets took over the 08.00 on June 17, 1991, but the name survived only three weeks into the electric era before disappearing on July 5.

THE TEES-THAMES

A SHORT-lived restaurant car train that ran from Middlesbrough and Saltburn to King's Cross and back. Normally hauled by Pacifics or V2s (and later by English Electric Type 4s), it left Saltburn at 7.05am and returned north at 2pm. The first run took place on November 2, 1959, and the last on September 9, 1961. It was preceded by 'The Tees-Thames Link' (see below).

THE TEES-THAMES LINK

ONE of the few DMU-formed service trains ever to regularly carry a headboard, the 'Tees-Thames Link' ran from Middlesbrough to Doncaster, so didn't even link the two rivers in its title. It operated for one summer only and in the southbound direction only. Its first run was on June 15, 1959, and its last on October 30 of that year, but it was not discontinued because it was unsuccessful. On the contrary, it proved the need for a loco-hauled train on the route and it was duly replaced by 'The Tees-Thames' (see previous entry).

TEES-TYNE PULLMAN

ALTHOUGH the 'Silver Jubilee' was never re-created after the war, a crack express was introduced on September 27, 1948, to run in its 5.30pm time slot as far as Newcastle. This was the 'Tees-Tyne Pullman', which had a slightly more leisurely schedule than the much-lamented "Silver Bullet" but had the benefit of being a full Pullman train.

It ran Mondays-to-Fridays and called only at Darlington, usually being hauled by an A4 or A1. In 1949, it was retimed to leave London at 4.45pm and from January 16, 1961, was re-equipped with new Metro-Cammell Mk1-based Pullman coaches. Its 1965 timing of 33 minutes for the 44 miles from Darlington to York made the express – by then 'Deltic'-hauled – the first in Britain to have a timetabled 80mph-plus schedule.

Despite that, the train became a mixed formation of

London Kings Cross

THE
TEES TYNE
PULLMAN

Durham • Darlington • Northallerton • York • Stevenage • London Kings Cross

Above: In the early 1960s, a new fleet of Pullman coaches was built by Metropolitan Cammell. The contrast between these and the old type can be seen in this illustration of A4 No. 60026 Miles Beevor *near New Southgate in July 1961, with the 'Tees-Tyne Pullman', the first vehicle being of traditional design.*

Left: When the 'Tees-Tyne Pullman' was resurrected as an HST working in 1985, this special adhesive 'headboard' was used for the relaunch. A SMITH

Pure 1960s: A3 No. 60036 *Colombo* on 'The Thames-Clyde Express' at Bingley Junction, Shipley, on May 10, 1961. Note the high position of the headboard. GAVIN MORRISON

Met-Camms and ordinary 2nd class Mk 2s in May 1969 and was withdrawn on May 2, 1976 – victim of a national recession.

The title was, however, resurrected by BR in the HST era and made history on September 27, 1985, when a Newcastle-King's Cross 'Tees-Tyne Pullman' demo run using an IC125 set a new world record for diesel traction when the 268 miles were reeled off in 2hr 19min 37sec.

The title survived into the Great North Eastern Railway era and wasn't officially dropped until 2004.

TENBY & CARMARTHEN EXPRESS

A GREAT Western Railway service, which was launched in 1928 and connected London Paddington with Tenby and Pembroke Dock, in south-west Wales.

"THE TEN O' CLOCK"

THIS was a popular nickname used in years-past to describe the 'Flying Scotsman', whose departure from King's Cross was traditionally 10am. It also referred, in LNWR days, to a Euston-Glasgow Central service that eventually became 'The Royal Scot'.

THAMES-AVON EXPRESS

LIKE the 'Regatta Express', the 'Thames-Avon Express' was an early example of a train title appearing in digital display form on the front of a Class 166 'Thames Turbo'.

Its first use was in 1994/5 for the 09.17 Paddington to Stratford-upon-Avon duty and subsequent timetables show a 17.31 ex-Stratford as a named up working. Use of the title continued until the year 2000.

THAMES-FORTH EXPRESS

ON the same day the 'Thames-Clyde Express' was launched, September 27, 1927, the LMS inaugurated a second named train from London St Pancras. But instead of running to Glasgow, this one's destination was Edinburgh and it therefore logically took the title 'Thames-Forth Express'.

However, whereas the 'Thames-Clyde' went on to become one of the country's best-known trains, its sister was fated to remain a virtual unknown.

'The Thames-Forth' shared the same Midland Main Line and Settle & Carlisle routes as far as Carlisle and then took the ex-NBR Waverley route into Edinburgh's Waverley

THE names of four trains linked the names of two rivers and oddly enough, they all started with the letter 'T'. A fifth example falling into that category was the 'Tees-Tyne Freighter' (see freight panel, p81).

The 'Thames-Clyde Express' was one of the few titled trains in the pre-preservation era to use the spectacularly scenic Settle & Carlisle line. Christened on September 26, 1927, it ran from London St Pancras to Glasgow St Enoch using the former Midland Railway route as far as Carlisle and then the ex-Glasgow & South Western Railway line via Dumfries.

Despite the challenging nature of the S&C, including the 'Long Drag' (15 miles at 1-in-100), the pre-war 'Thames-Clyde' was given just 51 minutes, pass-to-pass, to cover the 46 miles of the most difficult section, from Hellifield to Appleby.

BR restored the express's name after the war (the first

A black-backed version of the 'Thames-Clyde' headboard, seen on 'Royal Scot' No. 46103 *Royal Scots Fusilier*.

'Jubilee' 4-6-0 No. 45659 *Drake* has a red-backed version of the headboard in this view.

resurrected run being 22 years to the day since the very first titled run) and, in 1960, drafted in ex-LNER A3s to bolster the ex-LMS 4-6-0 fleet before 'Peak' Type 4 diesels began to make the service their own. The final run of this famous train was made on May 3, 1975.

(The up workings were reportedly known at one time as the 'Clyde-Thames Express' but no photographic evidence of this has been found.)

Thankfully, very few titled trains were involved in serious crashes, but the 'Thames-Clyde Express' came to grief at Blea Moor in 1952 whle being double-headed by No. 46117 *Welsh Guardsman* and a 4P 4-4-0. PETER ROBINSON

station. The service (9.15am down and 10.15am up) continued after the war, but the name was never reincarnated. Instead, BR elected to give the train another title altogether – 'The Waverley', but even that development didn't occur until June 17, 1957.

THAMES VALLEY LIMITED
A NAMED coined by Thames Trains in 1993 for the 06.45 Banbury-Oxford-Paddington 'Turbo' service. The name, which was displayed on the unit's digital destination panel, had been dropped by September 1999.

'THAMES SCOT'
A QUASI-official name for a short-lived service linking London Paddington with Glasgow and Edinburgh via Birmingham in the early Privatisation era.

THE THANET BELLE
A SHORT summer-only Pullman train named after an area through which it passed – the Isle of Thanet – and established between London Victoria and Ramsgate on May 31, 1948. It left London at 11.30 and called at Whitstable,

A bevy of beauty queens, including Miss Kent, attended the launch of 'The Thanet Belle' in May 1948.

Above: Very early British
Railways publicity for the
Southern Region's four
'Belle' trains. 'The
Thanet Belle' was given
prominence on the
brochure because it
was the newest.

Herne Bay, Margate and Broadstairs, returning at 5.05pm.
Patronage did not come up to expectations despite several
permutations of times and so it was decided after the 1950
season to add through cars for Canterbury East. As that city
did not lie in Thanet, the train was renamed 'The Kentish
Belle'. Its last run with its old name was on September 24,
1950.

THANET EXPRESS

THIS title was first introduced by the London, Chatham &
Dover Railway from October 1, 1896 and applied to the
10.45am from London Holborn Viaduct to Ramsgate
Harbour, although the balancing up service was un-named.
It continued in use until June 30, 1905.

In May 1912, the title was resurrected by the South
Eastern & Chatham Railway and applied to a 10.15 (Fri-
Sat) London Victoria-Ramsgate Harbour service until 1915.

Seven years later, the 'Thanet Express' made its third
entrance in the timetable when it was reintroduced in July
1921, although this time it was more of a collective
descriptive term for a batch of services, whose trains
gradually had their names removed during 1926/27.

THANET PULLMAN LIMITED

THIS train (sometimes referred to as the 'Sunday Thanet
Pullman') was introduced as a Sundays-only London
Victoria-Ramsgate Harbour service by the South Eastern &
Chatham Railway in July 1921, leaving London at 10.10am
and calling at Margate West, Broadstairs and Ramsgate
Harbour. Patronage was disappointing and, in 1931, the
title was formally discontinued (although it had ceased to be
used in practical terms for a couple of years).

A similar Pullman service, with the London departure
time changed to 11.30, was launched by BR Southern
Region after the war, but under a different name – see
'The Thanet Belle'.

THE TINTO EXPRESS

'THE Tinto Express' – which started life in 1904 as 'The
Upper Ward Express' – acquired its name in 1911 and
provided quick transit to Glasgow Central for business
residents in upper Lanarkshire.

Operated by the Caledonian Railway, it started from

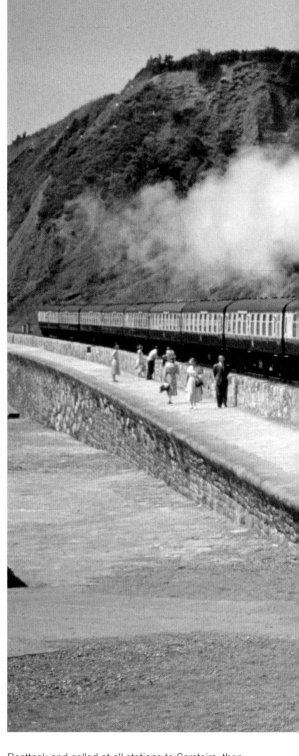

Beattock and called at all stations to Carstairs, then
Motherwell, returning in the evening. By 1934, the starting
point of the northbound service had moved south to
Lockerbie, while the evening return ran all the way through
to Carlisle.

The name of the train was derived from Tinto Hill, a
prominent mount near Symington, which was in view of
passengers for a considerable part of the journey.

(THE) TORBAY EXPRESS *

THIS train was known during the pre-war era by several
names, including the 'Torbay Limited' and the 'Limited
Express', but those were appellations in the timetable rather
than on headboards.

It was unusual in having an Ilfracombe slip portion that
included a restaurant car – believed to be the only such

slip coach operation in British railway history – and it was also notable in latter years for taking powerful 'King' class locos over the six-mile single-track section between Goodrington and Kingswear (now a preserved railway).

The train operated for the first time as a named service on July 9, 1923, with a London departure time of 11.50am (later changed to 12 noon) and eventually began running the 200 miles from Paddington to Torquay and Paignton in a shade under 3½ hours.

Officially, it was suspended in September 1939 for the duration of the war, but an eight-coach train leaving Paddington at 10.40 during the hostilities is known to have often borne 'Torbay Express' roofboards. A further five coaches were attached at Newton Abbot, but those didn't carry roofboards. On winter Sundays, the train ran via Bristol.

In May 1946, the title was officially restored and, 15

years later, a timetable change saw the London departure time altered to 12.30. In 1965, the title was transferred to a summers-only portion of the 'Cornish Riviera Express', which had been split off from the main 'Riviera' that year to form a separate train. The 'Torbay Express', with a new departure time of 10.50am, thus gained a further three years of life, but the name was dropped on September 13, 1968.

In 1983, the title was resurrected by British Rail and still runs as an FGW Paddington-Paignton HST, leaving Paddington at 10.00 and Paignton at 14.15 on weekdays and at 16.30 and 07.20 on Saturdays.

TORBAY-FORTH

THIS was the new name for the 'Severn-Tyne' after that service had been extended at both extremities in May 1971

A classic 1950s summer scene as 'Castle' No. 5079 *Lysander* and a ten-coach matching set of chocolate & cream Western Region coaches, forming the 'Torbay Express', skirt the Devon coast near Teignmouth on July 15, 1958. Holidaymakers stroll along the sea wall and a young enthusiast hoists himself up for a better look. R C RILEY

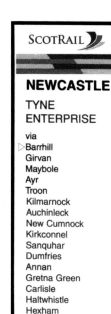

to run from Paignton to Edinburgh instead of Weston-super-Mare to Newcastle. A diesel loco-hauled service, it called at Newcastle, Birmingham, Bristol and Torquay. Like its predecessor, it is understood to have operated as a named train for only a year.

THE TORBAY-TYNE

A SHORT-lived Paignton-Newcastle service, inaugurated by BR in 1970, which left Paignton at 7.20am and Tyneside at 12.05pm. From May 1971, it was extended to/from Edinburgh but the title did not appear in the 1972 timetable.

TORQUAY PULLMAN

ONE of only two Pullman services operated by the Great Western Railway, the 'Torquay Pullman' was inaugurated in July 1929 and left Paddington at 11am, reaching Torquay, 194 miles distant, at 2.40 and Paignton, its terminating point, 10 minutes later. The up train left Paignton at 4.30 and arrived back in the capital at 8.30pm.

The Great Western's experiment with Pullmans was very short-lived and both this and the company's other Pullman venture (introduced on the London-Plymouth 'Ocean Liner' boat trains two months earlier) were withdrawn the following year, due to poor loadings. The cars were transferred to the Southern Railway.

(TRANS-PENNINE EXPRESS)

(*Brand name*): Not to be confused with the present-day train operating franchise of the same name, this was a title given by British Rail to its Liverpool-Hull service in the 1960s. The name has been mistaken in the past for a specific titled train, due to some of the Swindon-built six-car DMUs constructed in the early 1960s especially for the service (later Class 124s) having carried 'Trans-Pennine' headboards in the early days (picture, see p20).

TYNE ENTERPRISE

THIS train was unusual in bearing different titles for its out and back services. Introduced by BR's Regional Railways sector in winter 1989/90, the 'Tyne Enterprise' ran as one of the first 'Super Sprinter' services from Stranraer Harbour to Newcastle via Carlisle, while the balancing service in the opposite direction went under the title of 'Galloway Enterprise'. Both titles were dropped circa 1997.

THE TYNESIDER

A SLEEPING car train running between King's Cross and Newcastle Central. Inaugurated on June 5, 1950, it left London at 11.45pm and arrived at its destination at 6.03am, while the times of the southbound service times were 10.35pm and 4.35am. (Slumbering passengers were allowed to remain in their cabins until 7.30). As the train grew in popularity, the departure time of the down service

Above and right: A trio of rare photographs depicting the only known titled train to have run on the Isle of Wight – 'The Tourist'. It sported roofboards rather than a headboard and is seen, right, leaving Sandown behind E1 0-6-0T No. W3 *Ryde* on August 31, 1932. The carriage close-ups were taken on August 19, 1952, by NEIL SPRINKS. Main image: RAIL ARCHIVE STEPHENSON

THE TOURIST

THIS was a real rarity – a named train on the Isle of Wight.

One of Britain's shortest-distance standard gauge titled trains (the 'Ilfracombe Boat Express' and 'The Harrovian' were shorter), it was introduced, unofficially, as the 'East and West Through Train' by the Southern Railway in

1932, gaining its official title the following year. The name was carried on carriage destination boards.

The service ran from Ventnor to Freshwater via Newport, leaving at 9.55am and arriving in Freshwater at 11.12. The eastbound service departed from Freshwater at 9.20.

Engines were normally changed at

Newport, with E1 0-6-0Ts on the eastern section and A1 or A1X 0-6-0Ts usually working over the Freshwater leg. Some of the trains are understood to have included an observation car and, during a single week in summer 1933, a total of 2,700 passengers travelled on the service.

The title was discontinued in 1953.

was put back to 1am, but the up working retained its approximate schedule. 'The Tynesider' survived long enough to enjoy 'Deltic' haulage, but was withdrawn as a titled train on May 4, 1968.

THE TYNE-TEES PULLMAN

AS WELL as the famous 'Tees-Tyne Pullman', there was for a while a 'Tyne-Tees Pullman'. Operated by BR InterCity, its name was displayed in the windows of several King's Cross-Newcastle InterCity 225s in the early '90s.

THE TYNE TRADER

INTRODUCED by BR Regional Railways in winter 1989/90, the 'Tyne Trader' was the 06.45 Girvan-Newcastle service,

whereas the return 17.00 Newcastle-Girvan was known as 'The Ayrshire Trader'. The trains were related to the introduction of ScotRail's Class 156 'Super Sprinters', but both titles were dropped circa 1996/7.

THE ULSTER EXPRESS

IN the early Edwardian era, the Midland Railway was in expansive mood, acquiring the Belfast & Northern Counties Railway and building a major port at Heysham, Lancs, from which a steamer service ran to Belfast. To connect Heysham with London St Pancras, the MR laid on a train running via Lancaster, Hellifield, Leeds and Sheffield. Just along the coast, however, was the port of Fleetwood, from which two of the Midland's rivals, the LNWR and LYR, also ran train services to connect with Northern Ireland steamer services.

When all three railway companies came under the same LMS umbrella in the early 1920s, the new owners decided to cut down on the duplication. They elected to keep the MR's more modern port and the LNWR's more

Above and left: 'The Ulster Express' in the steam and diesel eras: 'Patriot' No. 45545 *Planet* on ex-LNWR metals circa 1960, and double-headed EE Type 4s led by D232 at Preston Brook tunnel, near Northwich in June 1963. *RM ARCHIVE, RAIL PHOTOPRINTS*

The rugged scenery of the Settle & Carlisle line provides the backdrop for this portrait of 'Jubilee' No. 45565 *Victoria* hauling the 'The Waverley' southbound under a threatening sky in the early 1960s. Painting by JOHN AUSTIN

Under the roof of its eponymous station, 'The Waverley' prepares to depart Edinburgh behind A3 No. 60099 *Call Boy*. RM ARCHIVE

THE WAVERLEY

THIS train began its named life in 1927 as the 'Thames-Forth Express', following a course that took it from London St Pancras to Leeds and then over the rugged lines of the Settle & Carlisle and the ex-NBR Waverley Route.

It wasn't resurrected by BR after the war and, by the time the year 1957 had arrived, it looked as though it wouldn't. But BR had another idea in mind – a relaunch coupled with a change of name to 'The Waverley'.

There were accelerated timings too, implemented on June 17 that year, and although progress was still relatively pedestrian through the Cheviot Hills and Yorkshire Dales, the Nottingham-London average was reeled off at a mile a minute.

The train ran happily with its new identity for 11 years but, by 1968, BR wanted to concentrate efforts on its better-known sister, the 'Thames-Clyde Express' and so, after a few months running as 'The Waverley Express', the former 'Thames-Forth' disappeared from the scene on September 28 that year, followed not many months later by the Waverley Route itself.

direct rail route. In July 1927, the LMS decided to confer a name on the boat train and 'The Ulster Express' duly came into being, although for the first year it continued to run to Fleetwood, Heysham not becaming the terminus until April 30, 1928.

With a departure from the harbour at 7am, the new train reached London Euston a full 1¼ hours faster than would have been the case if the longer Midland route had been chosen. The train's name and restaurant cars were removed during the war but brought back on September 26, 1949, and the train remained in use until the Heysham-Belfast boat service itself was shut down, on April 6, 1975.

THE UPPER WARD EXPRESS
THE name by which 'The Tinto Express' was first known.

THE VICTORY
THIS title was coined by Network SouthEast's South-Western division in 1989/90 for the 08.06 Portsmouth Harbour-Waterloo service and 16.50 return. It was named after Nelson's flagship *Victory*, which is preserved in Portsmouth, but proved considerably less robust than the vessel, failing to outlast the NSE era.

VINCENT VAN GOGH
THE number of train titles associated with Harwich Parkeston Quay over the years is well into double figures. This one, the 'Vincent van Gogh', ran cross-country to and from Liverpool in the early 1990s and was usually formed of a Class 158 DMU. Inaugurated as a successor to 'The Loreley' in 1992, it remained in service until May 1994.

'VIRGIN INVADER'
UNOFFICIAL name of a Virgin Trains Euston-Liverpool service, circa 2001. Not to be confused with 'Pendolino' set No. 390050, which has the same name.

WEEKEND PULLMAN
INTRODUCED on July 16, 1927 and not to be confused with other Harrogate Pullmans, this train ran from King's Cross to Harrogate via Leeds Central on Saturdays and returned south on Sundays.

Because the existing 'Harrogate and Edinburgh Pullman' also ran from King's Cross on Saturdays, the

---

VENICE SIMPLON ORIENT EXPRESS and THE BRITISH PULLMAN

THE 'Venice Simplon Orient Express' is a private luxury train linking London and Venice. It is popularly known as the VSOE or the 'Orient Express'.

The train was assembled in the 1970s and '80s by an American, James Sherwood, who spent almost £10m purchasing and restoring withdrawn (and often decrepit) Pullman and Wagons-Lits cars dating from the 1920s and 30s, thus enabling the first London-Venice run to be made on May 25, 1982.

The VSOE has separate carriages for use in the UK and continental Europe, with passengers being conveyed through the Channel Tunnel from Folkestone by coach on the Eurotunnel shuttle. The UK rake is known as 'The British Pullman' and is also used for charters and land cruises.

A companion train, the 'Northern Belle', operates mainly in northern England and Scotland.

(The modern-day VSOE services should not to be confused with the regularly-scheduled 'Orient Express', which was in operation in continental Europe between 1883 and 2009 and whose original route was Paris to Istanbul).

'Weekend Pullman' had its own set of Pullman cars. However, it did not last very long and was withdrawn after less than a year, on April 29, 1928, to be replaced the following weekend by the 'Harrogate Sunday Pullman'.

(THE) WELSH DRAGON (Y DDRAIG GYMREIG)
THERE were two quite distinct trains of this name. The first was believed to be the only steam-worked push-pull service on the UK main line to have borne a title and headboard. It shuttled daily in the summer between Llandudno and Rhyl, usually powered by an Ivatt 2-6-2T.

Usually comprised of only three coaches, it had another claim to notability insofar as its headboard was carried on the front of the leading carriage when the train was in 'push' mode.

Introduced in July 1950, it went on to be a surprisingly long-lived entity, surviving until summer 1970 – although long before then, it had been replaced by a DMU and rarely carried the headboard.

The second 'Dragon' was an altogether more glamorous beast. The title was resurrected by BR InterCity as the title for a London Euston-Holyhead express in

Left: Believed to be the only titled steam push & pull train in Britain, 'The Welsh Dragon' shuttled between Llandudno and Rhyl and is seen leaving Llandudno Junction behind ex-LMS 2-6-2T No. 41276 on July 26, 1962. ALAN BRYANT/*RM* ARCHIVE

Holyhead
Nuneaton—Crewe—Chester—
Rhyl—Colwyn Bay—
Llandudno Junction—Bangor

HOLYHEAD
Rugby – Nuneaton – Stafford –
Crewe – Chester – Rhyl – Colwyn Bay –
Llandudno Junction – Bangor

WELSH DRAGON

HOLYHEAD
Rugby – Nuneaton – Stafford –
Crewe – Chester – Rhyl – Colwyn Bay –
Llandudno Junction – Bangor

WELSH DRAGON
DDRAIG GYMREIG

LONDON EUSTON
Bangor—Llandudno Junction—Colwyn Bay—
Rhyl—Chester—Crewe— Lichfield Trent Valley—
Nuneaton—Watford Junction

Y DDRAIG
GYMREIG

The station shown in red has a short platform.
Take care when alighting.

HOLYHEAD
Rugby · Nuneaton · Crewe · Chester ·
Rhyl · Colwyn Bay · Llandudno Junction ·
Bangor · Holyhead ·

DDRAIG GYMREIG
WELSH DRAGON

LONDON EUSTON
Bangor · Llandudno Junction ·
Colwyn Bay · Rhyl · Chester · Crewe ·
Stafford · London Euston ·

THE WELSH DRAGON

LONDON EUSTON
Bangor · Llandudno Junction ·
Colwyn Bay · Rhyl · Chester · Crewe ·
Stafford · London Euston ·

Y DDRAIG GYMRIEG
THE WELSH DRAGON
INTERCITY
West Coast

Y DDRIAG GYMRIEG/THE WELSH DRAGON   *West Coast*

LONDON EUSTON
Bangor · Llandudno Junction · Colwyn Bay · Rhyl · Chester · Crewe ·
Stafford · London Euston ·

West Coast providing INTERCITY train services

LONDON EUSTON (Y Ddraig Gymreig/The Welsh Dragon)
Bangor - Llandudno Junction - Colwyn Bay - Rhyl - Chester - Crewe -
Stafford - Watford Junction - London Euston

1986, becoming one of the UK's few dual-language train names as it also featured the Welsh version – 'Y Ddraig Gymreig'. The branding then progressed through several slight changes, mostly resulting from changes of InterCity branding (see illustration above), before entering the Privatisation era for a short time under the Virgin Trains banner.

THE WELSHMAN (Y CYMRO)
A SUMMERS-only train that ran from London Euston to Holyhead, containing through carriages for Portmadoc and Pwllheli. Its first run as an officially-named train was on July 11, 1927 but was then suspended while war was raging, not being revived until June 5, 1950. The headboard was introduced the following year but was rarely carried. The

train appears to have disappeared from the timetable by the mid-'60s... however, the title was revived in 1985-88 for a loco-hauled service between Cardiff and Holyhead, which also used the Welsh language version of the name 'Y Cymro'. By 1990, the service had been renamed 'Provincial Express' and ran that year under that name but with a silver dragon logo.

(THE) WESSEX SCOT
A TITLE used by BR's cross-country sector between 1984 and 1997 to identify a service that varied over the years but basically ran from Dundee /Edinburgh/Glasgow to Bournemouth/Poole.

It was perpetuated by Virgin Cross Country until 2002.

WEST COAST POSTAL
THIS travelling post office is included because there were two periods – one in the Caledonian/ LMS era, and then again in the BR era between 1952 and 1967 – when its Aberdeen portion, of two to four vehicles, was attached to a passenger train at Stirling and run to Aberdeen as a combined rake. The combination arrived at its destination at 7.52am and the same arrangement applied to the up working, which departed for Stirling at 3.30pm.

The train starred in the famous GPO film 'Night Mail'.

WEST COUNTRY CAR SLEEPER
AN overnight train from Newcastle to Exeter St David's via Sheffield Midland, containing sleeping cars and covered car-carrying vans. Operated by British Railways in the 1950s, it used special car-loading and unloading docks at those three stations, starting at 5.45pm in Newcastle. A packed supper was provided at Newcastle and breakfast was served at Exeter while the cars were being driven off the train by railway staff.

WEST COUNTRY PULLMAN
A BR InterCity HST service between London Paddington and Paignton, which operated during the summer of 1988.

WEST HIGHLANDER
A SLEEPING car service run between London Euston and Fort William by BR InterCity in the early and mid 1990s. The title ceased to be used in 1996 and the train's modern-day equivalent is the 'Caledonian Sleeper'.
■ From 1984, the title had been used by BR for a summer timetabled (steam-hauled) service between Fort William and Mallaig, which was later renamed 'The Lochaber' and currently runs in the Privatisation era as 'The Jacobite', leaving Fort William at 10.15 with an additional train (departing at 14.30) between June 4 and August 31.

WEST MIDLANDS EXECUTIVE
AN INTER-City train run by BR (circa 1984-1990) from Euston to Shrewsbury, changing engines from electric to diesel en route.

THE WEST RIDING
ALTHOUGH the LNER and its BR successor decided not to resurrect the East Coast's three streamlined trains after the war, BR did launch a named service in 1949 called 'The West Riding'.

Of all the post-war trains, this one probably came closest to re-creating the magic of the pre-war streamliners, for half a dozen of the original coaches were

West Country CAR SLEEPER
NEWCASTLE
SHEFFIELD
Exeter

THE WEST HIGHLANDER
Sleeper
28 May to 23 September 1995
The West Highlander Sleeper Service between London and Fort William
INTERCITY
Sleeper

included in the formation (although of course, the on-board service would not have been of the same standard).

Starting on May 23, 1949, the train left King's Cross at 3.45pm and ran non-stop to Wakefield, continuing to Leeds Central, which was reached at 7.38. The southbound train left Leeds at 7.50am, although in November 1959, BR decided to turn the down service into a morning train, leaving the London terminus at around 7.50am.

The 'West Riding' became the first train to benefit from 'Deltic' haulage, in September 1961, but made its last run as a titled train on March 4, 1967.

(THE) WEST RIDING LIMITED *

THIS was the third and last of the LNER's iconic streamliners of the 1930s, although it lasted less than two years before the war rudely intervened.

As its name suggests, the train connected Leeds and Bradford with London and – continuing the theme of identifying A4s with each service – Nos. 4495 and 4496 were named *Golden Fleece* and *Golden Shuttle* respectively to reflect the Yorkshire woollen industry.

Inauguration day was September 27, 1937, and the eight-coach train comprised purpose-built articulated stock similar to that of 'The Coronation'. Unusually for a non-sleeping car titled train, departure from London was in the middle of the evening, at 7.10pm, meaning that arrival at Bradford Exchange was not until 10.15pm – a state of affairs not helped by the fact that the glitzy carriages had to be hauled over the last leg of their journey by tank engines, because of steep gradients at Leeds Central and Bradford Exchange, to which double-headed N2 tanks with their smaller wheels were more suited. The N2s also worked the southbound leg, leaving Bradford at 11.10am.

During the war, the coaches were stored inside Leeds Copley Hill carriage shed and although they were deployed thereafter (see 'The West Riding'), the train itself was never reinstated.

On December 2011, the title 'The West Riding Limited' was resurrected and applied to the East Coast train operating company's 06.30 weekday Bradford Forster Square to London King's Cross service, although the return journey is currently un-named. The revival was said by East Coast to be "in response to substantial public demand" and represented the reintroduction of a train-naming policy by the TOC. As part of the relaunch, Class 91 No. 91117 was renamed *West Riding Limited* on September 14, 2011, using nameplates featuring traditional LNER Gill Sans lettering.

WEST RIDING PULLMAN

NOT to be confused with 'The West Riding' and the 'West Riding Limited', the 'West Riding Pullman' pre-dated both. Its inaugural run was on July 11, 1927, although it had been running without a name since September 21, 1925.

Southbound, it ran from Harrogate and Leeds Central to King's Cross, but northbound it terminated at Leeds (continuing to Harrogate as empty stock until May 1, 1928, when passengers began to be conveyed all the way). There was a portion for Bradford, later extended to Halifax.

On July 9, 1928, the main train itself was extended to Newcastle Central (yet kept its name), reverting to Harrogate in September 1935, when it also began to detach/attach a portion for Hull at Doncaster. Because the train was now serving the East Riding as well as the West,

'The West Riding': A1 60117 *Bois Roussel* bursts from Welwyn North tunnel, April 1954. BRIAN MORRISON

'The West Riding Limited': A4 No. 4489 *Dominion of Canada* at Leeds Central in 1939. COLOUR-RAIL

'The West Riding Pullman': C1 class Atlantic No. 4436 near Greenwood in 1933. NRM.

its title was no longer considered suitable and the LNER renamed it the 'Yorkshire Pullman'. The last run under the old name was on September 28, 1935.

WEST YORKSHIRE EXECUTIVE

A SHORT-lived BR service running between London King's Cross and Leeds in 1984-85.

THE WEYMOUTH WIZARD

MOST railtours are organised by private charter companies and run on a one-off basis, but occasionally a railway company will choose to operate a limited service itself, usually for holidaymakers, and such trains have tended to run for several weeks or even a whole season.

An example in BR days was 'The Weymouth Wizard', which ran in the early 1980s between Swindon and Weymouth. In 2011, the Trans-Wilts Rail Group took steps to reintroduce the train on a trial basis.

THE WHITE ROSE

THE large cities of Leeds and Bradford have long been good sources of income for the East Coast companies and when BR came into existence, it decided to add a titled service to its series of West Riding operations.

The pair of trains so honoured with the name of a traditional Yorkshire emblem in May 1949 were the 9.18am from King's Cross and 5.15pm from Leeds Central (times that varied in later years).

With the help of Pacifics, and later Type 4 and 5 diesels, the service was gradually accelerated until reaching mile-a-minute status in 1963. The following year, however, the name 'White Rose' was transferred to the 'Queen of Scots' (which had been cut back from Scotland and so could no longer continue with

its original title, running for the last time under that name on June 13.

The (new) 'White Rose Pullman' took over two days later and continued running between King's Cross and Leeds/Harrogate until March 6, 1967 when its stock was commandeered for a new service – the 'Hull Pullman' – created by turning the Hull portion of the 'Yorkshire Pullman' into a separate train.

The 'White Rose' title was briefly reinstated by BR to describe a Swansea-York train in 1990/91 and then revived again (arguably as a brand) between 2000 and 2005 to describe a King's Cross-Leeds service operated by Great North Eastern Railway using Class 373 'Eurostar' sets.

Above: One of the most artistic styles of headboard was that of 'The Weymouth Wizard', a summer-dated train that ran between Swindon and Weymouth in the early 1980s. It is seen on Class 47 No. 47124 on July 12, 1984. RICHARD MORETON

Calm before the storm: A1 No. 60122 *Curlew* rests on King's Cross shed before flying north with 'The White Rose' in March 1958. COLOUR-RAIL

Left: In classic period postcard style, 'The Wild Irishman' is depicted at speed over water troughs in a 19th century setting on the LNWR main line. The name of the train is written in the bottom right-hand corner of the picture.

TITLED TRAINS OF IRELAND

ALTHOUGH a number of British trains bore names with Irish connections (e.g. 'The Emerald Isle Express', 'The Northern Irishman' and the "Wild Irishman" - see picture on right), Ireland also had a number of such trains of its own. The following is just a selection:

THE AMERICAN MAIL
BELFAST EXPRESS
BUNDORAN EXPRESS
CLADDAGH EXPRESS
CU NA MARA
DERRY EXPRESS
THE ENGLISH MAIL
ENTERPRISE
THE FAILTE
THE FESTIVAL
KILLARNEY EXPRESS
NORTH ATLANTIC EXPRESS
PORTRUSH FLYER
THE SAIRSEAL

summer, the length of the Stratford portion having earlier been reduced to three coaches.

Its chances had not been helped by the fact that printing of the summer timetable was delayed that year and it didn't appear until July 2, meaning that the service was advertised nationally for little more than two months.

The last run was on September 8, 1951, making this one of the shortest-lived regular titled trains of all.

THE YORKSHIREMAN

NOT to be confused with 'The South Yorkshireman', which was a product of the BR era and ran over ex-Great Central metals, this train was launched by the LMS in March 1925 and used the Midland Main Line route.

Linking London St Pancras with Bradford Exchange, it received its name shortly after its inauguration and ran for a decade despite competition from LNER trains connecting the same two cities. It was unusual for a Midland route Bradford service in that it did not run via Leeds. Instead, it picked its way through the complex of West Riding lines via Thornhill and Royston in order to access the Midland Main Line at Sheffield. By the late 1930s, the start times were 9.05am from Bradford and 4.55pm from the metropolis, but the service was one of many brought to a premature end by the outbreak of war.

British Rail reprised the title, but it disappeared again at the end of the 1977-78 timetable.

THE WHITE ROSE PULLMAN

A SHORT-lived King's Cross-York service that appears to have run under that title only in 1992. Before that, the name had referred to the former 'Queen of Scots' between 1964 and 1967.

'THE WILD IRISHMAN'

A SEMI-official name used by the London & North Western Railway in the 19th century to describe an express that carried the American mails from London Euston to Holyhead, en route to Dublin and Queenstown. The train, which was illustrated on several Victorian era postcards complete with its name (which today would doubtless be considered 'politically incorrect'), was a favourite of American travellers leaving or joining Atlantic liners at Queenstown.

THE WILLIAM SHAKESPEARE

THIS was one of two titles (the other was 'The Merchant Venturer') introduced by the Western Region of BR to mark the Festival of Britain in 1951.'The William Shakespeare' identity was bestowed upon the 10.10am Paddington-Wolverhampton and 7.50pm Birmingham-Paddington, which began running as named trains on the day the festival opened – May 3, 1951.

The title alluded to the fact that a four-coach through portion for Stratford-upon-Avon was detached at Leamington Spa and returned to that junction as the 7.23pm from Stratford.

The through portion was usually worked by an ex-GW Prairie tank – providing the rare sight of a tank loco bearing a headboard and creating another unusual situation, insofar as the main part of the express became (visually at least) anonymous between Leamington and Birmingham/Wolverhampton due to transfer of the headboard to the tank engine.

Despite being provided with brand-new BR Mk1 rolling stock and despite the potential for attracting American tourists to Shakespeare's birthplace, the train did not prove a commercial success and was withdrawn after just one

Below: With its three-line plate seeming even larger perched above the smokebox door of Prairie tank No. 5163, the Leamington portion of 'The William Shakespeare' waits at Stratford in 1951. Note how the loco is still in GWR livery more than three years after Nationalisation. NRM

Main picture: The 'Yorkshire Pullman's new Metro-Cammell Pullmans are seen to good effect in this view as A1 No. 60141 *Abbotsford* powers through West Yorkshire scenery in the early 1960s.
GAVIN MORRISON

(THE) YORKSHIRE PULLMAN

THIS name came into being on September 30, 1935 as a result of a decision by the LNER to add a Hull portion to the 'West Riding Pullman'.

Because the train would thus serve the East Riding as well, a new name with a wider remit was necessary. The pre-war 'Yorkshire Pullman' normally loaded to eight coaches (four from Harrogate via York, two from Hull and two from Halifax), but it later grew to as many as 12, normally requiring Pacific haulage.

After suspension during the war, the train was reinstated on November 4, 1946, leaving Harrogate at 10.20am and London at 3.50pm, but it had no sooner got back into its stride than a national fuel shortage in 1947 saw it suspended again, this time until October 6 of that year. By the early BR era, the Hull portion had doubled to four cars and the start time from London had changed to 5.30pm.

The arrival of 'Deltics' and other diesels onto the East Coast saw the 'Yorkshire Pullman' begin to benefit from the new form of traction from the early-1960s, especially after it was re-equipped with new Met-Camm cars in January 1961, and, by 1967, Leeds was being reached in 3hr 10mins.

The train survived until May 5, 1978 – the day the last two Pullman trains were withdrawn from the ECML pending the introduction of HSTs – but the name was resurrected by BR in 1995 for a King's Cross-Leeds service that lasted into the Privatisation era, ending in 2004.

THE YOUNG EXPLORER

THIS was the name of the 09.00 Fort William-Glasgow Queen Street and 14.50 return between July 6 and September 5, 1992, and again (with slightly amended times) in summer 1993. For the 1994 season, the train was replaced by 'The Centenary Explorer'. The Scottish Region printed adhesive window labels for it, depicting a Class 156 'Sprinter', but the train was locomotive-hauled… so BR staff carefully snipped the DMU picture off all the labels!

'ZEEBRUGGE CONTINENTAL'

PASSENGERS from London Liverpool Street to Harwich Parkeston Quay for summer ferry sailings to Zeebrugge in GER/LNER days usually travelled on 'The Antwerp Continental', but, on occasions, separate trains were provided for them. It is understood that these may have been unofficially named 'Zeebrugge Continentals'.

THE ZEPHYR

COMMENCING operations in December 2007, open access operator Grand Central gave this name to its 06.46 Sunderland-King's Cross service, reflecting the American styling of the company's logo. The name applied only to this train, the down working at 16.50 being called 'The 21st Century Limited' (see next column). The name lasted only a few months and had been dropped by the start of the December 2008 timetable.

'THE ZULU'

THIS unofficial name was applied to two separate trains. One was a broad gauge Paddington-Plymouth express put on by the Great Western Railway in 1879 – the year of the Anglo-Zulu war.

With a departure time from London of 3pm, (11.15am

from Plymouth), it had a timing almost identical to that of the 'Flying Dutchman', thus giving the GWR two 'flyers' whose timings were claimed at the time to be unequalled in the world… although in March 1891, the down train didn't fly anywhere as it was trapped in a snowdrift in south Devon for four days.

The second service to bear 'The Zulu' name operated in standard gauge days; the 11.47am Birkenhead-Paddington and 4.45pm return. Again, however, it appears to have been an unofficial title.

THE 21ST CENTURY LIMITED

THIS was the title of Grand Central's 16.50 King's Cross-Sunderland service, the balancing turn in the opposite direction being called 'The Zephyr'. Although based on a long-running American express, the name was very short-lived, being dropped by the start of the December 2008 timetable.

Please direct any amendments, queries or comments on this publication to: Nick Pigott, Editorial offices, Media Centre Mortons Media, Morton Way, Horncastle, Lincolnshire LN9 6JR. Email: npigott@mortons.co.uk

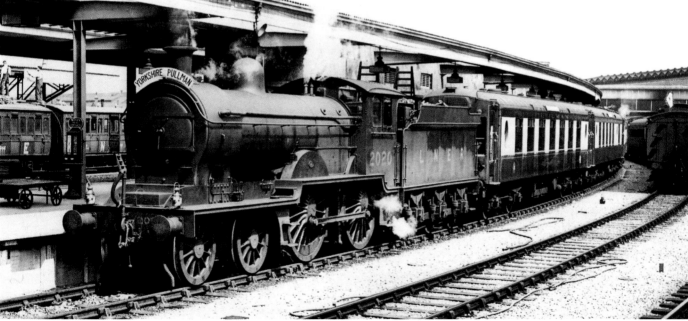

One of the LNER's graceful high-steppers, Starbeck-based 4-4-0 No. 2020, waits at York station with the Harrogate portion of the 'Yorkshire Pullman' in the summer of 1938.

Bringing up the rear

In steam and early modern traction days, several named expresses bore their title on the rear as well as the front:

'The Royal Scot'

The 'Bournemouth Belle'

'The Silver Jubilee'

'The Caledonian'

And, appropriately last...
The 'Golden Hind'

Finally, a light-hearted picture to end our journey. The crew at the Wissington Light Railway in the 1940s clearly had a sense of humour, attaching this basic home-made headboard to the bunker of their humble tank engine. For many tens of thousands of railway employees over a century and a half, however, titled trains were indeed their 'bread and butter'!

THE DEMISE OF TITLED TRAINS

A NUMBER of developments have combined to kill off the majority of titled trains. In no particular order (and not all relevant to the present day), they are:
■ The introduction from the 1970s of identical standardised, fixed-fomation train sets, such as HSTs – all capable of the same performance and all able to fill in on any turn on their diagram at short notice, thereby making them unsuitable for enhanced exterior or interior treatment
■ The deployment of long-distance units such as 156s, 158s, 'Turbostars' and 'Voyagers' on what would previously have been locomotive-hauled formations.
■ The establishment of an improved regular-interval service and increased use of standardised or clockface departure times.
■ The withdrawal of Pullman cars.
■ The phase through which British Rail passed in the late 60s/early 70s when corporate image was a principal aim.

■ The unsuitability of modern traction for the affixing of headboards or roofboards – plus a desire to eliminate delays caused by the fixing of such artefacts at the start of, or during, a journey, especially in an era of quick turn-round times.

Given the above, it may be thought that in today's multiple unit-dominated network, it would be impossible to replicate the attachment and detachment of through trains, which was one of the great features of long-distance expresses in steam days.

Yet such couplings and uncouplings still take place on Network Rail (at Northampton, for example, where the London Midland TOC still splits some eight-car sets from Euston and runs them forward to Birmingham as four-car trains).

The 'Caledonian Sleepers', too, are worth taking a journey on, for they are the closest surviving relatives of multi-portioned trains such as 'The Atlantic Coast Express' and the 'Cornish Riviera Limited'.